"Renita Weem's book, *Just a Sister Away*, is one that I am compelled to give to the women in my family and urge the men to read. It is for both.

"Easily read, *Just a Sister Away* does not conceal the careful biblical scholarship of the writer. Without preaching, she communicates a powerful message of 'women pooling their resources, sharing power, forging alliances, building bridges among themselves' for the purpose of enriching life for all. Her message transcends racial, cultural, and economic barriers, appealing to our justifiable pride in our womanhood and challenging us to strengthen the spiritual and moral values of our own day through mutual support, which is both our common heritage and our present opportunity."

> *Leontine T. C. Kelly, Bishop, California-Nevada Conference of The United Methodist Church*

"The womanist imagination of Renita Weems brings the biblical women to new life, whereas her personal reflection connects them with women's struggles today. The study questions for group discussion highly recommend the book for Bible study groups."

> *Dr. Elisabeth Schuessler-Fiorenza, Talbot Professor of New Testament Studies, Episcopal Divinity School, Cambridge, Massachusetts*

"Renita Weems offers all who are open and sensitive a penetrating and, at times, disturbing re-reading of Scripture. In her hands, the Bible cries out as never before. We are challenged to face feminist insights which have the ring of awesome, undebatable truth, even though her vision may make us long for the calmer days now revealed as willfully ignorant in their innocence."

> *Dr. Ella P. Mitchell, Dean of Sisters Chapel, Spelman College, Atlanta, Georgia*

JUST A SISTER AWAY
by Renita J. Weems

*A Womanist Vision
of Women's Relationships
in the Bible*

Innisfree
Press, Inc.

*A call to the
deep heart's core*

Copyright © 1988 Innisfree Press, Inc.
Philadelphia, Pennsylvania
International Copyright Secured
Printed and Bound in the United States of America

Innisfree Press, Inc.
136 Roumfort Road
Philadelphia, PA 19119-1632

Library of Congress Cataloging-in-Publication Data
Weems, Renita J., date.
    Just a sister away : a womanist vision of women's
relationships in the Bible / by Renita J. Weems.
      p.   cm.
      Bibliography: p.
      ISBN 0-931055-52-0 (pbk.)
      1. Women in the Bible   I. Title.
BS575.W39   1988   88-8084
220.9'2'088042—dc19   CIP

The Scripture quotations in *Just a Sister Away* are the author's own translations from the Hebrew and Greek Bibles.

To my mother, Carrie Baker Weems, (1932–1984)
who, in light of her sorrows,
I now know needed a sister more than a daughter.

CONTENTS

FOREWORD

Just a Sister Away was written for those of us who are hungry. If you are like myself, you have heard and read about many of the women in the Bible all your life, and you have often wondered whether there might not be another way of understanding their stories. Those biblical women whose stories have gained the attention of the Church are renowned either for being thoroughly selfless or resolutely wanton. Such amblyopic interpretations infer that, in the sight of God, women must be notoriously one or the other.

Dutifully, we have sat through sermons, lectures, and Bible study lessons, nodding when appropriate, copiously taking notes when expected and, when called upon, obediently recapitulating what we have been told. All the while our souls have remained starved for a new revelation on the role of women in salvation history. Surely, God did not mean for us to be a footnote to redemption.

A fiction writer whom I greatly admire once disclosed that she tries to write the kind of books she would like to read. *Just a Sister Away* was written to be just that kind of book for myself — and for you. It is, I imagined as I wrote it, the kind of book which irascible women, hungry for stories of women they can recognize and a God they can trust, could snuggle up with and rejoice when reading.

And if, like myself, you are an African-American woman, you are all the more hungry to hear a voice you recognize. How many times have I gone into bookstores — feminist, African-American, and Christian bookstores — desperately seeking a book written unapologetically with me, an African-American woman, in mind. When I have made purchases, it is because I, like so many, have learned how to redesign what I can and to make do with what I have. Although there has been a recent groundswell of literature by and about black women in the non-religious sector — and we all benefit greatly when black women regain their voices — the voice of black women religious writers has been strangely muted. Therefore, *Just a Sister Away* was written unapologetically with African-American women in mind as a way of reminding us that we are not an afterthought to salvation, that the first step toward satisfying the gnawing hunger within us is to pick up a pencil.

Just a Sister Away attempts to combine the best of the fruits of feminist biblical criticism with its passion for reclaiming and reconstructing the stories of biblical women, along with the best of the Afro-American oral tradition, with its gift for story-telling and its love of drama. For this reason, the novelist Alice Walker's term "womanist" — referring to a black feminist; a courageous woman who is committed to *whole* people, both men and women — best describes the critical perspective taken here. That is, *Just a Sister Away* is an *audacious* attempt to probe beneath the surface of biblical texts to discover a place for everyone in the Kingdom. The intent is to explore the uncharted territory of stories that could give us clues as to what biblical women felt about their lives.

We know all too well how ancient men felt about women; and we have a reasonably sound idea of the role of women in ancient society, home, synagogue, and church. But how the women felt about themselves, we do not know.

What we do know is that one of the best ways to get an idea of how a woman feels about being a woman is to take a look at how she treats other women. Hence, *Just a Sister Away* examines women's relations with one another.

Of course, to let the women speak for themselves, I have had, from time to time, to wrestle these nine stories from their presumably male narrators. What has emerged are creative reconstructions of the *possible* emotions and issues that motivated biblical women in their relations with each other. The assumption is simple: despite differences in time, culture, lifestyles, attitudes, biblical women were compelled by the same passions as we — love, compassion, hope, jealousy, and fear. A common thread of sacred female experiences continues to bind centuries of women. While these reconstructions of the relationships between women in the Bible make no claim to fact, they do claim to be responsible and realistic testimonies of the ways in which women sometimes perfectly, other times imperfectly, love themselves and one another.

In Bible study groups, women's gatherings, workshops, and over coffee, dialogue is (or should be) taking place among women about the issues that affect us most: our faith, our families, our frustrations, and our futures. For those interested in seeing how ancient women worked out their faith, *Just a Sister Away* will help facilitate those discussions. Since its inception, *Just a Sister Away* was conceived as a resource tool and study guide for women; hence, the questions after each story are designed to call attention to the parallels between the plight of biblical women and women today; and to prod us to tread the deeper waters of our faith by forcing us to grapple with the tangled skein of issues and emotions that confront us as women today.

Finally, the writing and publication of *Just a Sister Away* are themselves a testimony to the peculiarity of female bonding. I wish to thank the host of women I have met at workshops and worship services; friends who have encouraged me with gifts (in particular, Ms. Annie V. Taylor of New York) and humor; my editor Marcia Broucek and publisher Lura Jane Geiger who gently, but firmly prodded me; and the great cloud of ancestral witnesses who hovered over me until I, with the succor of the Holy Spirit, agreed to take the first step toward satisfying my own hunger.

Renita J. Weems
Lent, 1988

𝔸 MISTRESS, 𝔸 MAID, 𝔸ND ℕO MERCY

Read: Genesis 16:1-16; 21:1-21

For black women, the story of Hagar in the Old Testament book of Genesis is a haunting one. It is a story of exploitation and persecution suffered by an Egyptian slave woman at the hands of her Hebrew mistress. Even if it is not our individual story, it is a story we have read in our mothers' eyes those afternoons when we greeted them at the front door after a hard day of work as a domestic. And if not our mothers' story, then it is certainly most of our grandmothers' story.

For black women, Hagar's story is peculiarly familiar. It is as if we know it by heart.

The easiest thing in the world would be to make a case out of the ethnic differences that separated Hagar and Sarai — differences today which would manifest themselves between an African woman and a Hebrew woman, a woman of color and a white woman,* a Third World woman and a First World woman.

---

*Certainly, ancient people were aware of one another's color (e.g., in Song of Solomon 1:4, the writer, presumably referring to his skin color, speaks of himself as "dark and comely"; and in Numbers 12:10 it was as much that her skin turned "white as snow" as it was that Miriam was a leper that the narrator felt deserved comment.) But there is no evidence that race and color, as we understand them today, especially as a way of stratifying people, prevailed at that time.

Concentrating on the ethnic differences that separated these women would be easy.

But it would not be totally fair to make the Old Testament story of Hagar and Sarai carry all the weight of the history of race relationships in the modern world. Yet the similarities between the biblical story and the reality of the relationships across racial lines among women today are undeniable. Like our own situation, the story of the Egyptian Hagar and the Hebrew Sarai encompasses more than ethnic prejudice. Theirs is a story of ethnic prejudice exacerbated by economic and sexual exploitation. Theirs is a story of conflict, women betraying women, mothers conspiring against mothers. Theirs is a story of social rivalry.

Hence, the similarity of our stories, as black and white women in America, to the story of Hagar and Sarai warrants taking the enormous risk of opening up the deep festering wounds between us and beginning to explore our possibilities for divine healing.

The biblical story opens with the spotlight on Abram's barren wife, Sarai (Genesis 16:1).* The first thing we come to know about Sarai, other than her status as Abram's wife, is the stark fact of her barrenness. In ancient times a woman's self-worth and social status pivoted around her family — namely, the reputation of her husband and, more importantly, the number of children she had borne, preferably males. Therefore, the first verse of the chapter is especially significant; in that one line Sarai's honor rises and falls:

---

*The progenitors of the nation of Israel are introduced in the Genesis narrative (Genesis 12) by the names of Abram and Sarai. The two are known to us by those names until Genesis 17, at which time we are told that God entered into covenantal relationship with them, changing their names to Abraham and Sarah to symbolize their new relationship with God, to signify the sealing of the covenant with the birth of a son of their own.

Therefore, all discussion of the events in Genesis 16 will refer to the two by their pre-covenant names, Abram and Sarai. When the story turns to Genesis 17, the discussion will refer to the couple as Abraham and Sarah.

"Now, Sarai, Abram's wife, bore him no children" (Genesis 16:1).

As the wife of Abram, who was a socially prominent and successful herdsman, Sarai was a wealthy woman in her community. As a Hebrew mistress, she was a woman of immense social and economic standing. But Sarai was barren. And in the culture in which Sarai lived, a woman's womb was her destiny.

In a world devoid of the technological skills which we in the Western world have come to take for granted; in a world where entire families, communities, and nations could be wiped out by famine, drought, plague, and pestilence without warning; in a world where the average life span of men was forty years and women, thirty years; in such a world, the ability to reproduce and replenish the population was held in high esteem. Thus, despite her marriage to Abram and all the social and economic privileges that came with such a union, Sarai's barrenness made her a woman to be scorned.

As is the case with most wealthy women, however, Sarai possessed a handmaiden. Hagar, the Egyptian slavewoman, attended to the personal and domestic needs of her Hebrew mistress. While her mistress was old and had no hope of ever conceiving a child, Hagar was young and fertile. But Hagar was poor. In fact, she was worse than poor: she was a slave. And because she was a slave, Hagar was powerless. The differences between the two women, therefore, went beyond their ethnic identities, beyond their reproductive capabilities. Their disparities were centered in their contrasting economic positions. And economic differences have, on more than one occasion, thwarted coalitions and frustrated friendships between women.

With the scant information contained in the first verse alone, we have all the clues we need to know that this story will probably end in sadness.

Sarai, the barren but wealthy mistress, appealed to her husband, Abram, to go in and have intercourse with her fertile but poor handmaiden, Hagar. The child born to that union would become Sarai's. After all, Hagar was Sarai's property; what belonged to Hagar actually belonged to Sarai.

Sarai had social standing, as Abram's wife, but she had no respect. She had material abundance, but she was not comforted. She was beautiful, but she was barren, childless, less than a woman in the eyes of her Hebrew community. That which Sarai craved most, her husband's money could not buy her. Only her slave's womb could give it to her. And according to custom, because Hagar belonged to Sarai (through Abram, of course), any children Hagar bore would legally belong to Sarai. Thus, what the Lord had prevented of Sarai, Sarai set out to obtain through her slave.

Notice: The slave Hagar was never asked her opinion.

Without so much as a murmur of protest, Abram complied. Hagar conceived.

To our modern way of thinking, Sarai's act of giving Hagar to her husband, Abram, as a concubine is nothing less than reprehensible. We are offended not only because of our moral and legal customs concerning monogamy and fidelity, but we are also offended because of the seeming presumptuousness of it all. The nerve of Sarai exploiting Hagar's body, manipulating Abram, speaking for God!

Yet we must lay aside our cultural biases long enough to consider that Sarai was not the only woman in the Bible to convince her husband to have sex with another woman. Rachel, too, persuaded her husband, Jacob, to enter into conjugal relations with her maid Bilhah (Genesis 30:1-24). Not only was concubinage an acceptable custom of the times, but there were men who took concubines evidently with their wives' blessing. At least for barren women, concubinage functioned in a critical way to provide a (male) heir who would retain land and property holdings within the family.

However, providing an heir for her husband's immense property was not Sarai's sole concern. Sarai (as did Rachel, no doubt) had her own reasons for offering her slave to Abram.

> *"Perhaps I will be esteemed through her"*
> *(Genesis 16:2).*

Through her slave's womb, Sarai sought esteem and honor for herself.

But the tables were turned on Sarai.

> *"But when Hagar saw that she had con-*
> *ceived, her mistress' honor was lowered in*
> *her eyes" (Genesis 16:4).*

Instead of esteem, Sarai received contempt. Instead of respect, Sarai was ridiculed. And by her maid, no less!

Whether Hagar's contempt for Sarai was real or imagined on Sarai's part, we can only guess. (After all, the story is told more from Sarai's point of view than Hagar's.) But one thing is certain: Hagar's elevation as Abram's pregnant concubine must have served only to point up Sarai's downfall as the wife who could bear him no children.

As the woman carrying the child of the wealthy landowner, the status of the pregnant slavewoman in the house of her mistress and master drastically changed. The relationship between the mistress and maid required renegotiation. Before, Hagar had been a defenseless slave. Now, as the pregnant concubine of the prosperous but old man Abram, Hagar was protected. She ceased to be Sarai's slave and became Abram's wife.

Perhaps the pregnancy awakened something in the slavewoman, something that previously lay dormant.

Perhaps it was her sense of self-worth.

Perhaps it was her sense of purpose and direction.

Or, perhaps, it was the prospect of being loved unconditionally by her child. (Pregnancy has had that effect on
more than one woman.)

Whatever the reason, Hagar could no longer see Sarai
and her relationship to her mistress in the same way as
before, for Hagar was able to give the old man Abram
something his wife Sarai could not. Consequently, Hagar
transformed before her mistress' eyes. Her attitude about
herself changed as well. The child growing inside her was
proof that she was more than a slave: she was a woman.

Resentful and enraged, Sarai renounced her part in the
whole humiliating affair (Genesis 16:5). She blamed Abram.
He, in turn, renounced his authority, role, and interest in
the irksome situation and gave Hagar back into the hands
of Sarai to be done with as she saw fit. Thus, as quickly
as Hagar was elevated to the position of wife in her mistress'
house, she was reduced back to the position of slave. She,
who had been to Abram as a wife through a transfer of
power, once again became property — again, without her
permission.

Once Sarai's authority over the pregnant slavewoman
was restored, the barren wife proceeded to punish the
slavewoman for humiliating her: she began to treat Hagar
harshly. We know only too well the kinds of violence the
Egyptian woman must have been forced to endure: beatings,
verbal insults, ridicule, strenuous work, degrading tasks,
and the like. For to be under the power of a resentful woman
can be a dangerous thing.

If we as black women appear, to some, to be reading
too much of our own brutal history into the biblical story,
let it be pointed out that whatever the nature of the punish-
ment Sarai imposed, it was evidently harsh enough to convince the slavewoman to run away. Hagar chose the
unknown dangers of the wilderness over her pallet in her
mistress' house.

The story of the Egyptian slave and her Hebrew mistress is hauntingly reminiscent of the disturbing accounts of black slavewomen and white mistresses during slavery. Over and over again we have heard tales about the wanton and brutal rape of black women by their white slavemasters, compounded by punitive beatings by resentful white wives who penalized the raped slavewomen for their husbands' lust and savagery.

There are also the pitiful stories of slavewomen who willingly conceded to their slavemasters' sexual advances: first, as a way of protecting their husbands, children, and loved ones from being beaten; second, as a way to keep themselves and those close to them from being sold away; or, third, as the only way of elevating their social rank in order to protect themselves from vicious overseers and mistresses.*

The painful memory of black and white women under slavery and the web of cruelty that characterized their relations continue to stalk the relationships between black and white women in America even to this day. Slavery was abolished in America a mere one hundred twenty-five years ago; but evidently one hundred twenty-five years is not long enough to abolish the memories and attitudes that slavery arouses in a nation. Unless a miracle occurs, it is sad to say that it will probably take another one hundred twenty-five years to erase the pain and antagonism bred from two hundred fifty years of the cruelest brutality one race could inflict upon another — especially in the name of God.

And, for some peculiar reasons, when it comes to women, those memories have proven especially hard to erase.

---

*Some of the more popular and recent collections of slavewomen's testimonies have been recorded in *Black Women in Nineteenth-Century American Life*, by Bert Lowenberg and Ruth Bogin (University Park, PA: Penn State University, 1976); and in *We Are Your Sisters: Black Women in the Nineteenth Century*, edited by Dorothy Sterling (New York: W.W. Norton & Company, Inc., 1984). For an especially poignant fictional account of slavery based on real testimonies, see Margaret Walker's *Jubilee* (Boston: Houghton Mifflin, 1966.)

Resentment and distrust linger. For black women in America, there remains the fear that white women, if given the slightest opportunity, will betray their trust and exploit their vulnerability as racially and sexually oppressed women. And with good cause: in many instances modern history, too, has borne out these suspicions.

In the second half of the nineteenth century, suffragettes, who began their social activism as ardent opponents of slavery and race prejudice, eventually used racism to secure their right to vote. They pandered to the racist attitudes of white southerners who ardently opposed black enfranchisement, and they extolled the supremacy of white women over black men (and black women).*

More recently, white women within feminist and Christian feminist circles continue to speak as though theirs is the universal experience. In doing so, they betray their persistent belief in their superiority and sovereignty over women of other races.

The truth is, very few black women manage to make it through adulthood without a footlocker of hurtful memories of encounters with white women.

A recent odious experience comes to my mind and, I admit, continues to grieve me. I was invited by a group of white women to join them in planning an upcoming national symposium. Because their stated objective was to see that this symposium, unlike previous ones, be multi-ethnic, they were eager to solicit the input of black women on their otherwise all white board. At first when asked, I flatly declined. Admittedly, I am immediately suspicious of requests for my services primarily because I am black, and when I can help it, I try to avoid being the only black in otherwise all white settings. Both, as I see it, portend

---

*For a very helpful discussion of the similarities in the racism within the nineteenth century suffragette movement and that within the modern feminist movement, see Barbara Andolsen's *Daughters of Jefferson, Daughters of Bootblacks: Racism and American Feminism* (Macon, GA: Mercer University Press, 1986).

danger. However, after much persuasion and insistence upon the sincerity of this group's intentions, I consented.

At the first meeting, everyone was very enthusiastic and solicitous of the other black woman and myself. In fact, our suggestion for the theme of the conference was accepted unanimously. The next time the group convened, however, it was a closed session — without either of the two black women having been invited. For days I walked around hurt and enraged. Again and again, I berated myself for betraying my instinct and for allowing myself to be used once again by white women. Every time I saw the announcements for the upcoming symposium with the title I had suggested, I wanted to scream.

But, as I said before, the story of Hagar and Sarai is about more than ethnic prejudice. It is not fair to make this Genesis story carry all the weight of race relations between black women and white women in the modern world.

In the first place, owning slaves was not unique to the ancient Hebrews. Later, in the book of Exodus, we discover that the hands of power reversed: Hebrew women became slaves in the hands of Egyptian women. (It would become the responsibility of an Egyptian Princess to come to the rescue of a Hebrew slavewoman.) In other words, no race or culture has a monopoly on evil. At some point in its history, virtually every culture has, if not instituted slavery, then profited from the bartering of human flesh.

In the second place, the story of Hagar and Sarai is about the economic stratification of women as much as it is about the ethnic discrimination of one woman against another. Translated into today's language, Hagar was a domestic; Sarai was her employer.

Certainly there is nothing inherently ignoble about being a maid, nor anything inherently honorable about being an employer of a maid. Neither need apologize nor boast. Circumstances and lifestyles have a lot to say about the choices we make. Women who have been in the position to do so have long sought the help of other women in maintaining the physical upkeep of their households. Women who have had to do so have long hired themselves out for the one line of work many have known since childhood. The problem lies not with the choices themselves, but with the attitudes that too often accompany the choices.

Within a capitalistic society such as our own, disparate economic relationships among women can distort perspectives of reality. Among the "haves," it breeds a false sense of superiority. Among the "have-nots," it breeds an irrepressible sense of inferiority. Wherever human worth and dignity are measured by purchasing power, there is always the problem of class prejudice.

In the instance of Hagar and Sarai, the owner took advantage of her economic leverage over the Egyptian slavewoman. She exploited the slavewoman's body for her own personal ambitions. But in trying to provide a son for her husband and secure respect for herself, Sarai almost lost a slave. And that would never do!

When she saw that her scheme had backfired, Sarai tried to save face and regain her (false sense of) superiority over Hagar. She tried to humiliate the slavewoman and, thereby, remind Hagar that it was she, Sarai, who had power — not Hagar. In so doing, Sarai grasped desperately for the little power her husband had restored to her hands, even if that power extended only to slaves.

Taking advantage of Hagar's slavewoman status, exploiting the fact that the woman who tended to her house was vocationally limited and her financial options virtually non-existent, Sarai took advantage of her status over Hagar. She knew that the way to enslave a slave — all over again — was to humiliate her, to destroy her (new found) sense of self-worth, to dehumanize her.

It works every time.

Not all women in America have had the means, temperament, or need to employ the services of a domestic. Neither have most women ever deliberately exploited another woman economically. But practically all of us in capitalistic America have found ourselves in situations where we have been grievously reminded of the inequity among people in general, and women specifically.

I am the daughter and granddaughter of domestics, and the great-granddaughter of a slave. Yet through freak circumstances and the grace of God, I am an educated and employed black woman upon whom, from time to time, capitalism confers the opportunity to exploit other women — both black and white. My potential victims are those who are neither educated nor employed.

I am painfully aware of this when I step across the floor recently mopped by the black janitress at the office building where I am late for an executive meeting. This fact becomes glaringly evident when I eat out at a restaurant, and the white waitress who is the age of my mother calls me "ma'm." And I am reminded of my privileges when, while sitting at a desk in my hotel putting the final touches on a speech for an organization of Christian women, the Latina maid tiptoes in to replace my soiled linen and make my bed.

None of us is safe from the ravages of a society which makes room for only a chosen few and keeps at bay the vast majority. For those of us who are educated and employed, there is always the potential to be a Sarai; and, lamentably, there are far too many opportunities in a capitalist society for her to surface. Yet most of us are just a paycheck away from Hagar.

The tragedy of it all is that, in actuality, this is neither Hagar's nor Sarai's story. It was never meant to be. It is

Abram's story. The episode concerning Hagar and Sarai is only part of a larger drama about the promises of God to God's elected servant Abram. Hagar and Sarai are introduced only in so far as the role they play in being used by God to demonstrate the faithfulness of the divine promise to Abram: the promise that God would grant to Abram a legitimate heir who would, in turn, be a blessing to the nations (Genesis 12:1-3; 17:1-4).

As Abram's wife, Sarai proved to be unfaithful and too impatient to trust God's promise to her husband. She lost sight of who she was in relation to the sovereign word of God, and in so doing, she lost sight of reality itself. Sarai forgot that in a patriarchal society she and her female slave Hagar had more in common as women than that which divided them as Hebrew mistress and Egyptian slave-woman. In fact, the only things which separated the two women were a couple of cattle and some sheepskins (which in today's language translates to a paycheck and a diploma). What bound them as women in Abram's house — their fate as women in a society that seemed to reward only men — also brought them back together.

If we are committed to the whole truth, we cannot dismiss Hagar's participation in this story. Notice her pathetic sense of herself. In many ways, by acting as a passive victim throughout, she participated in her own exploitation. We admire her for her courage in getting out of the abusive relationship with Sarai (Genesis 16:6). But we are disappointed that in the end she did not have the wherewithal to remain gone. Hagar did not even have the strength to define herself.

Upon finding Hagar at a spring in the wilderness (Genesis 16:7), the angel of the Lord asked the runaway slave the unavoidable question:

> *"Hagar, maid of Sarai, where have you come from; and where are you going?"* (Genesis 16:8).

Hagar was not only broken, she was empty as well, too empty to seize her future. From whence she had come, she was all too aware:

> *"I am fleeing from my mistress..."* (Genesis 16:8).

But *where* she was headed, unfortunately, Hagar could not answer. She could not answer because, although she had run away, she still understood herself to be a slave: "...my mistress..." And to a slave, life without a mistress is inconceivable.

Hagar's body was free, but her mind remained in bonds. What Sarai thought of Hagar had become what Hagar thought of herself: she was property.

Could it be that the angel had no other choice but to send the runaway slave back to the reality in which she had defined herself? The Egyptian woman was part free and part slave. She had fled, signaling her desire to be free, yet she had to return to her mistress' house because she continued to see herself as a slave. Therefore, the angel commanded her:

> *"Return to your mistress and submit to her"* (Genesis 16:9).

Hagar's blessing was within her reach, but beyond her grasp.

When we meet the two women again in the story (Genesis 21), Hagar had given birth to Abram's slavechild,

Ishmael. She had resumed her servitude in that household. Sarah, in spite of herself, had conceived and given birth at last to a son of her own — Isaac, the legitimate heir of Abraham — just as God had promised. However, the friction between the two women had not lessened; it had only heightened.

This time, threatened by the relationship developing between the two lads and fearful that the slavewoman's son might upstage her son's inheritance, Sarah convinced her husband to evict the slavewoman and Ishmael. Reluctantly, Abraham complied. Saddling a skin of water and some morsels of bread upon Hagar's shoulders, Abraham sent the woman and their child away to make it the best way they could.

Before, Hagar had left voluntarily. This time, she was banished by her son's father. Once more she found herself in the wilderness alone, destitute — only this time with a hungry, crying child to care for. But God found her where she was and opened her eyes.

Yet before God was forced to intercede on the slavewoman's behalf, there was a woman who could have made a difference in Hagar's situation. One word from Sarah that afternoon, as Abraham saddled up Hagar and Ishmael, could have made a difference in Hagar's story.

Even though Sarah might have sorely regretted her husband's previous relationship with Hagar and resented the child born out of that union, and even though she might have been sorry for her part in the entire sordid affair, Sarah, nevertheless, could have spoken a word to remind her husband that his responsibility to the Egyptian woman and their child went beyond water and a few crumbs of bread.

We must remember this story for its piercing portrayal of one woman's exploitation of another woman.

Quite frankly, the kinds of atrocities some mothers have committed against other mothers and their children continue to stun me. I am often amazed at the extent to which otherwise intelligent, otherwise moral women (and men) will renounce intelligence and morality to protect some perceived rights they feel their children have in relation to other mothers' children.

I am reminded of the sight of scowling, rabid mothers picketing and yelling vile insults at innocent school children whose only offense is that they have been infected with the AIDS virus and want to continue to go to school. Then, there is the sight of white mothers from Little Rock, Chicago, and Boston snarling and hurling obscenities at innocent black children en route to schools they have been forced by the courts to desegregate. What is there about these children that these women hate so much? What kind of fear is this that explodes into madness? I doubt whether the day will ever come when I am no longer appalled by human evil.

Perhaps, on the other hand, Sarah was right. Perhaps it was best for everyone involved for the slavewoman and her child to leave Sarah's house. (Sometimes we need a shove — even from our enemies — to make us stand on our two feet.) But there is a difference between a shove and a kick. Surely Hagar deserved more than morsels from her former mistress, and even more from her son's father. Sarah, despite her disdain for the situation, could have come to the slavewoman's defense. She could have encouraged her husband to make better provisions for his son — at least.

Instead, Sarah thought of her own security and that of her own son, Isaac. God had shown mercy to Sarah by granting her a child from her own womb. But Sarah was not willing, in turn, to show mercy to a woman whose back was up against the wall.

Sarah had used the woman for her own purposes, but she would not condescend to speak up on behalf of the evicted woman in her hour of abandonment.

Had Sarah forgotten so quickly what it felt like to be rejected and scorned?

Not only would she not help Hagar, but Sarah also conspired against the Egyptian woman. She preferred to let a few morsels replace genuine mercy.

Can we deny the sorrow in this story? Can we afford to ignore the lessons of this kind of pain? The answer to both questions is a resounding "No." The story of Hagar and Sarah touches us in the many places we hide, places which are not often held up for public view. It is a story which also exposes the many hidden scars and ugly memories of the history of relationships between racial ethnic and white women in America.

But the story is not limited to the races. It goes beyond race and speaks to the class stratification that divides women: the so-called "professional" woman versus the so-called "non-professional" woman; the female Young Urban Professional (YUPPY) versus the female factory worker; the Black Urban Professional (BUPPY) versus the store clerk.

Hagar and Sarah's story searches out our unconfessed sins of arrogance and low self-esteem, presumptuousness and passiveness, jealousy and faithlessness, and our conspiracies to get others to do for us what we cannot do for ourselves. Like an endless row of braids, the plot weaves the strands of so many women's lives together. And Hagar's life becomes the braid of the oppressed and rejected women — from the exploited maid and the welfare mother, to the single mother and the pregnant girlfriend.

Moreover, if we can step outside of the painful memories that haunt us in our relationships racially as black and white women, and economically as stratified women, we might find another story, one equally familiar, one equally haunting. We will recognize it by its basic storyline: two women's involvement with the same man.

Hagar's and Sarah's story is also the story of the "other woman" by whom a man has children. In many cases this woman is the most abused, neglected, and maligned woman of us all. We, like Sarah, think if we can ignore her children, we can also ignore her.

At some time in all our lives, whether we are black or white, we are all Hagar's daughters. When our backs are up against a wall; when we feel abandoned, abused, betrayed, and banished; when we find ourselves in need of another woman's help (a friend, neighbor, colleague, relative, stranger, another man's wife); we, like Hagar, are in need of a woman who will "sister" us, not exploit us.

In those times we are frequently just a sister away from our healing. We need a woman, a sister, who will see in our destitution a jagged image of what one day could be her own story. We need a sister who will respond with mercy. We need a sister whose genuine mercy — not pity which is episodic, random, and moody — is steadfast, consistent, and free.

Betrayal. Exploitation. Denial. Resentment. Suspicion. Distrust. Anger. Silence. How do we get past these memories? How do we reach beyond the enormous gulf of distrust on both our parts and forge friendships and coalitions?

It will not be easy.

In fact, it will be very difficult.

It will require a deliberate effort on our part to listen when it is easier to dismiss.

At times, it will mean that we must be as willing to confront and confess the evil in us, as a community of women, as we are to point to evil in the world.

It will require a resolve to work with one another both in spite of and because of the pain.

It will require a willingness to respect the genuine differences in one another and to see them as the strength of our coalition, not the bane of our existence.

As black and white women in America, as Israeli and Lebanese women, as white South African and black South African women, as Asian and European women, as the wives of terrorists and the wives of victims of terrorists, working for righteousness in splendid isolation from one another is a luxury we cannot afford.

Injustice in our lands relies upon the perpetual alienation of women from one another and upon relentless hostility between women. Indeed, our estrangement from one another continues to compromise the integrity of our witness as God-fearing women.

The future of our families depends upon our ability to bridge over the memories of our scars.

The future of our people depends upon our willingness to tunnel through the tragedies of our past encounters.

The future of our world depends upon our resolve to walk headlong into that which makes us different as diverse tribes of a vast world and to march straight into that which binds us as people of God.

If we don't, who will?

Finally, out in the wilderness, overcome with grief, the bitter, distraught, banished Egyptian slavewoman set her child down and went off a short distance to weep alone. She could not bear to watch her son suffer.

This time, instead of an angel, the Lord appeared. However, it was not the mother's weeping which caused the Lord to speak. Rather, it was the child Ishmael's tears that moved the Lord to intervene on behalf of the mother, Hagar.

> "But the Lord heard the voice of the lad"
> (Genesis 21:17).

Just as Ishmael must have wept for the senselessness of Hagar, Sarah, and Abraham's ways, maybe it will take our children weeping on our behalf — our children weeping for the sins and prejudices and stubbornness of we their mothers and fathers — to convince God to intervene on our behalf. Perhaps as a global community we will be saved — if we are to be saved at all — because of the little children whose innocent tears will prostrate heaven.

Though their tears have not always moved us, hopefully they will move God.

God have mercy upon us.

Questions for Thought

1. How would you evaluate the relationship between black and white women in America today? Black and Latina women? Protestant and Jewish women? How does our shared faith in Jesus Christ (or God) help ease the differences between us or help erase the memories of what has taken place in the past between us?

2. What has been your most painful encounter with a woman from another racial/ethnic background? Were your differences related to your ethnic/racial backgrounds, or were they economic or political in nature? Or were they simply differences in personalities? How, if at all, did the two of you resolve your differences? What has been your most positive encounter with another woman from a different background?

3. In what ways can women from differing ethnic/racial/national/economic backgrounds bind together and significantly impact global politics and religious controversies?

4. Is the relationship between a domestic and her employer necessarily hostile? How do the dynamics of that relationship change when the domestic and her employer are the same race and/or age?

5. What examples can you point to that have made you aware of the economic differences between you and other women? Have these differences concerned you, and if so, how do you deal with them?

6. Examine the divine appearances to Hagar the two times she was in the wilderness (Genesis 16 and 21). In the final analysis did Hagar ever receive a blessing from God, and if so, how? Was she ever vindicated, and if so, how? Is vindication important?

7. In the case of surrogate mothering (where one woman pays another woman to have a child for her, and the biological mother renounces all rights to the child she bears) what are the Christian considerations? What, at present, is our counsel to women who are unable to bear children?

8. What are our responsibilities as women to our brothers and our sons who take no responsibilities for the children they have sired? As wives whose husbands may have children by other women, what are our responsibilities to our husbands' other family? How do you feel about these responsibilities?

BLESSED BE
THE TIE THAT BINDS

Read: The Book of Ruth

I remember my first encounter with a grieving widow. She was a member of my church, and I knew her only slightly. Her reputation as a fine artist brought me to her home one Sunday afternoon to discuss working on an upcoming project together. Her husband of some twenty or more years had died less than a year before, and I had been warned by well-meaning mutual friends that she was consumed with his memory.

They were right.

I found myself that afternoon with a woman I hardly knew, pouring over a photo-album full of pictures of a man I had never met, listening to her recount over and again their courtship, the details of their twenty years or so of marriage (without children), their good times and bad, their disagreements, his idiosyncrasies (*always* his precious idiosyncrasies), and the dreadful details of his fatal heart attack.

When appropriate, I laughed with her and oohed, and when otherwise, I cried with her and shook my head. Several times she wondered out loud how she was going to make it without him. But most of all, I listened...which was all she wanted from me, a friendly, patient ear. Many of her friends from church had grown weary of the endless stories. Others, like myself, were embarrassed by tragedy, and so they avoided her and let a kiss on the cheek or a wave across the church parking lot suffice.

From time to time in the midst of her monologue, this woman would look at me and remember that I was a virtual stranger and plead, "Forgive me, I know you don't want to hear about all of this." When I would assure her that I did want to listen and that I had planned nothing else for the day (not exactly true), she would continue her story without missing a beat — grateful, I suspect, that I was willing to listen.

Although we accomplished very little on the project I had come to talk about, I did not begrudge the time I spent with her. I knew I had been in the presence of a woman who was unapologetically in love. . .which was a welcome relief from being around women I knew who had lost their ability to love. The only problem was that the man whom this woman loved was dead, but not her love for him. Her husband was dead, but her capacity to love and receive love had not diminished.

"What is this woman supposed to do with all this love," I found myself questioning that afternoon, "now that he's gone?" I listened and listened and listened, and thought of the story of Ruth and Naomi.

Ruth and Naomi's story is especially refreshing because it is a story of friendship between a woman and her grieving mother-in-law. Their friendship is a welcome contrast to the numerous other stories in the Bible which portray women competing against one another for status, power, and men: Hagar and Sarah, Rachel and Leah, Miriam and her sister-in-law, to name a few.

Ruth and Naomi's story is one of the oldest testimonies in the Old Testament to female bonding. Their relationship typifies the special friendship that can often develop between women, despite differences in age, nationality, and religion. Ruth and Naomi's legacy is that of a seasoned friendship between two women, a friendship which survived the test of time despite the odds against women as individuals, as friends, as women living without men.

The Hebrew woman Naomi is introduced through her husband Elimelech (Ruth 1:1). A famine in their homeland of Bethlehem had forced Elimelech to take his wife and their two sons, Mahlon and Chilion, and relocate in the distant land of Moab (present-day southwest Jordan) where food was not as scarce. No sooner had they arrived in the land of Moab, than Elimelech mysteriously died. His wife, Naomi, was left with the task of raising their two sons alone in a foreign land. As sons eventually do, Mahlon and Chilion in time grew up, left the protective care of their widow mother, and took wives for themselves — Ruth and Orpah, two Moabite women.

Ten years passed, and Mahlon and Chilion also died, leaving their widows childless and alone. Soon afterward the three widows — Naomi and her two daughters-in-law, Orpah and Ruth — pooled their meager resources to eke out a living together. Without children in their lives to fill that gnawing hollow space known only to widows, Orpah and Ruth had only their aging mother-in-law to keep alive the memories of their deceased husbands. Likewise, Naomi, bereft of her husband and two sons, had only her two foreign daughters-in-law to comfort her.

The three widows lived together in Moab as a household of women bound together by their mutual love for and memories of the same dead men. However, when Naomi heard that her God had eased the famine back in Bethlehem, she set out to return to the land of her foremothers, accompanied by Orpah and Ruth.

But somewhere between Moab and Bethlehem, Naomi changed her mind about taking Orpah and Ruth with her. It was not fair, she thought, to ask the two young women to give up the familiarity of their homeland in exchange for the unknown of Naomi's homeland. Besides, Orpah and Ruth were not hers to take with her; that which had belonged to Naomi was buried back in Moab.

> "Go, return each woman to her mother's house. And may the Lord show you stead-fast love as you have shown the ones who are dead and me" (Ruth 1:8).

Although Naomi was grateful for the devotion of her daughters-in-law over the years, she chose to send each one back to her own "mother's house." Naomi was entirely too old and too barren to mother them any longer. She had too many strikes against her: she was a woman alone in a world defined by male relationships, and she was old. Since she had neither a dowry nor an inheritance to offer, Naomi felt she had nothing more to give.

For all practical purposes, Naomi was as good as dead — or so she thought. She even referred to herself as ". . .the dead and me." But in spite of her own loss, Naomi wished only the best for the Moabite women and offered a blessing of appreciation for her daughters-in-law:

> "May the Lord grant that you find a resting place, each woman in the house of her husband" (Ruth 1:9).

Unlike Naomi, Orpah and Ruth were still young women, healthy and attractive enough to look forward to building new lives for themselves. They still had a chance to remarry and have children. The same could not be said for Naomi; she was too old for lust and breastfeeding. The older woman surrendered the young women into the hands of the Lord with her prayer that God would do for them what she could not. Her farewell kiss brought a flood of tears.

Orpah and Ruth protested: the Moabite women refused to return to their homeland. Naomi was the only mother they had known for a long time, and they insisted upon following her to the home of her foremothers.

While the devotion of her daughters-in-law impressed Naomi, it also depressed her. After all, what had bound the three of them together was what her womb had had to offer. Now that she was old and her childbearing days over, what else did she have to give? A woman with a withered womb, no sons, and a dead husband was of no use to anyone, particularly young women. She could only be a burden to them. Even the Lord had abandoned her, she argued (Ruth 1:13). Again, the women wept.

This time, Orpah heeded her mother-in-law and turned back. But let us not judge Orpah too harshly. Her decision to return to her home was not one of disloyalty; it was one of common sense. Perhaps there was a future for her back in her mother's house, with her people. Orpah opted to trust the wisdom of an old woman rather than the sentimentality of her young heart. Following the suggestion of her mother-in-law, Orpah agreed to choose another path and, in so doing, terminated a good relationship that had gone as far as it could — even though the love between the two women continued to live.

But not everyone can — nor wishes to — go home again. In contrast to Orpah, Ruth clung to her mother-in-law and refused to leave her. Ruth's words have become a part of eternity:

> "Do not urge me to abandon you nor to turn from following after you. For where you go, I will go. Where you lodge, I will lodge. Your people will be my people, and your God, my God. Where you die, I will die. And there I will be buried. May the Lord do to me, and even more, if anything, save death, separates me from you" (Ruth 1:16-17).

Ruth's words are so uncompromising in their commitment, so resolute in their pledge, they embarrass us. They are not, as we have adapted them, words spoken between a woman and a man, pledging faithfulness to each other in holy matrimony. Rather, they are the words of one woman to another woman, the younger woman pledging herself to the older in a testimony of sisterhood, committing herself to serve, care for, and stand by the older woman, in spite of what lay ahead.

Naomi and Ruth could never return their former relationship to one another: mother and daughter-in-law. The men they had once shared, the men responsible for bringing them together, were now dead. Their new relationship would have to reflect their new realities. Perhaps they could give friendship a chance. Ruth committed herself to a woman who, for all practical purposes, had nothing to give her in return. The young Moabite woman was willing to give up her right to a family — a husband and children — to follow an old woman to a strange land.

Yet Ruth's commitment to Naomi was not out of some morbid attachment to the dead. Five times in her pledge, Ruth repeated the pronoun "you," each time emphasizing her commitment to Naomi. It was not her dead husband's memory to which Ruth clung, but rather the good friendship with Naomi which she did not want to lose. Ruth was not interested in what Naomi's womb could or could not offer. Her pledge was to Naomi, the woman. It was Naomi whom Ruth had grown to love and care for.

The two women had seen each other through a lot.

In return for her relationship with the older woman, Ruth expected a people and a god. Naomi and her kinsfolk would become Ruth's family, and Naomi's God, Ruth's God. Despite Ruth's pain from the loss of her beloved husband, despite the feeling of alienation she would soon know in a foreign land, she did not choose to return to her former life. Unlike her sister-in-law Orpah, Ruth elected to build on the bonds she had already established and to risk love again.

Before such unrequited devotion, Naomi was speechless.

Notice: In the darkest moments of the story — when Naomi was bereft of husband and children, when Orpah and Ruth were bereft of their husbands, when the women had to decide whether or not to abandon one another — no angel of mercy came to the women's defense. No divine messenger offered counsel to the bewildered. No God came with words of wisdom and assurance. Naomi, Orpah, and Ruth were left to the integrity of their faith and the strength of their relationship with one another. The women had to make their own decision, without the help of intervening powers.

One woman decided to go back. One opted to go forward. One sunk into despair.

Eventually, the Hebrew woman and the Moabite woman made their way from the plains of Moab to the harvest of Bethlehem (Ruth 1:19). When the townswomen of Bethlehem saw their long-lost friend, unsure of this faded image of a friend once-known, they queried among themselves, "Is this Naomi?"

Naomi overheard their whispers, and her depression edged into bitterness:

> *"Never again call me 'Naomi.' Rather, call me 'Mara' for the Almighty has treated me bitterly"* (Ruth 1:20).

Naomi renounced the name her mother had given her; its meaning, "liveliness and delight," no longer suited her. "Mara," meaning "bitterness," more appropriately described her situation. Indeed, the Almighty had taken from her everything which gave meaning and status to a woman's life in her society, namely her husband and children.

Uncomforted by the presence of the young woman who had accompanied her throughout the long journey — a woman who had given up everything to follow the older woman — Naomi reminded her kinswomen that she had left the barren land of Bethlehem some years back in fullness. She had had a family then, and thus a future. Now she had come back home empty, bereft of husband and sons. All she had to show for her life was the strange devotion of a Moabite woman.

Before such inconsolable depression, this time it was Ruth, not Naomi, who was speechless.

Nonetheless, Ruth was not discouraged by her friend's grief. Ruth had made a commitment to Naomi, a commitment to look beyond her friend's bitterness to see her loneliness.

This is the first commandment of friendship: to be a sister to a friend even when she is neither in a position nor disposition to reciprocate the sisterhood.

Ruth had promised, back on the plains of Moab, to be Naomi's friend if Naomi wanted, to be a daughter when Naomi needed. But Naomi, consumed with grief over her loss and despair about her future, was unable to reciprocate the friendship. To the young woman's credit, Ruth did not deny Naomi the right to grieve.

It was the persistent love of Ruth's friendship which helped bring about Naomi's healing.

Ask any woman who has lost her husband, and she will tell you that a widow's mourning is eventually interrupted by reality. Soon, she is forced to suspend the grieving process long enough to focus her attention on the matter of how she will survive when mourning has passed.

Naomi and Ruth were no exceptions.

Naomi, however, was too old to provide for herself; thus the responsibility for taking care of the two of them fell squarely on Ruth's shoulders. But economic responsibility did not become Ruth's excuse to dominate Naomi. Because the greatest need in her friend's life was the need to be needed — the need to mother a child and to be loved unconditionally — Ruth, in spite of her economic edge over Naomi, continued to defer to her older friend as her elder (Ruth 2:2).

Time passed and Naomi began to show signs of her healing, signs of letting go of the sorrow and depression that had once given her lonely life meaning. She found a new purpose for her life through Ruth. Despite the fact that Ruth was younger and therefore physically stronger than the older woman, Naomi was the wiser of the two. Naomi knew what it meant to be a woman in Israel. She also knew that their future together as women sharing a home depended on their mutual cooperation. Thus, in exchange for Ruth's work in the fields as a gleaner where she gathered up food for the two of them, Naomi instructed the younger woman in what was expected and permitted of her as a woman in a Hebrew society.

Gradually, Ruth began to occupy the place in Naomi's heart once filled by a husband and sons. Each woman, in her own way and at her own pace, reached out to the other, nurturing when called upon, mothering when necessary, sistering when needed. They eventually found the healing power of God in each other's love and forbearance. As it so often happens — if we are patient — in time the two women, who were once strangers, became friends.

And sometimes, just sometimes, a friend, a sister in a time of need, can make all the difference in the world.

What do you remember about your first female friend?

Perhaps she was your third grade teacher whom you loved for the way she would write her name every morning across the board without a slant, and for the smell of Jergens lotion on her hands as she braided your loose pigtail.

Perhaps she was your best friend from the sixth grade, the two of you sharing everything from pencils to peanut butter sandwiches to paper dolls. To seal your love for one another, maybe you pricked your index fingers, pressing one bleeding finger next to the other's, swearing loyalty to each other eternally as "bloodsisters."

Or perhaps your first female friend was the woman in the next project complex whom everyone else thought was "crazy," but whom you loved, both for the sound of the "Somebody-done-done-me-wrong" songs she sang as you scratched her head and for the dime she gave you when you ran to the store for her snuff.

Perhaps those first female friendships were uncomplicated, undistracted friendships.

Uncomplicated, because you had not yet learned how to ask more of your friend than she could give. A warm smile and the smell of Jergens on your teacher. . .a stale sandwich and a handy fist in the time of trouble from your best friend. . .a sad song and a dime from your neighbor. . .these simple offerings were enough to earn your fierce loyalty.

Undistracted — because despite what everyone else said, you never noticed that your teacher was nearsighted. . . that your best friend's hair was never combed. . .that your neighbor talked to herself — you loved each one for who she was and for what she consented to give you in your time of need.

Have you ever observed how this kind of love and loyalty between friends gets misplaced as we get older? We grow up and take our friends for granted, forgetting our histories together.

But Ruth was intentional in her efforts to preserve a good friendship.

Interestingly, as strong as their love for each other grew to be, neither Naomi nor Ruth was interested in living in a world without men. Their love for one another did not diminish their ability to love others. Conversely, Ruth's eventual love for Boaz did not result in her belittling or taking for granted her friendship and love for women in her life.

Still, the story about Ruth and Naomi and their female bonding goes further than we suppose. It certainly goes beyond the immediate interests of the narrator who recorded the story of Ruth and Naomi. As we see from the way the Book of Ruth ends, the narrator was interested in explaining how a Moabite woman, a foreigner, came to be the great-grandmother of the most renowned monarch in Israel's history, King David (Ruth 4:18-22). According to the narrator, Ruth's faithfulness and unwavering devotion to a Hebrew woman earned her a coveted place in Israel's history. And the narrator was absolutely right — in part.

On the surface, the Book of Ruth *is* about Ruth's eventual marriage to Boaz and the subsequent birth of their son Obed, the grandfather of David. But the story is also about faithfulness, devotion, commitment, and stubborn loyalty — the stuff that good relationships are made of.

The story of Ruth and Naomi is about two women who saw each other through a lot, two women who walked each other through the good times and the bad: marriage, the death of husbands and children, relocations to strange lands, poverty, courtship, remarriage, and births.

However, unlike many stories of shared good and bad, the good fortune that one woman experienced did not become the misfortune of the other. Ruth's marriage to the prosperous landowner Boaz did not signal the end of her friendship with the woman she had clung to in poverty. Ruth remembered the promise she had made to the older woman when there was no one but she and Naomi in the wilderness. She also remembered the role Naomi had played in advising her during her courtship with Boaz. Consequently, Ruth's blessing of husband and child became Naomi's blessing of a family and a future. Each woman found in the other's loyalty and companionship the future they thought they had lost in Moab.

To care passionately about the quality of another woman's life, to respect each other's choices, and to allow for each other's differences: these are the lessons embedded in the Book of Ruth.

For those of us who ponder this story, our vision is likewise to take seriously the quality of our relationships with the women and men in our lives. To refuse to be forced to choose between two good relationships — a romantic partnership with a man and a sustaining friendship with a woman — can be the story behind not only Ruth's, but every one of our lives.

Questions for Thought

1. What does friendship mean to you? What kind of women attract you as friends? What kind of women do you avoid?

2. What other stories in the Bible which portray friendships between women are most meaningful to you? What makes these stories important to you?

3. What stories in the Bible which portray friendships between men are most meaningful to you? Are there friendships between men whom you know which are similar to the friendships described in the Bible? In what ways, if at all, do friendships between men differ from friendships between women?

4. Have you ever had a friendship with another woman which approximated Ruth and Naomi's story, a friendship where the two of you saw each other through a lot of good and bad times, and still remained friends? What was your friendship like?

5. Have you ever taken advantage of a friendship? Have you ever felt that your friendship was being taken advantage of? What has your experience been in these situations?

6. Have you ever been in a very close relationship with a woman that changed significantly when one of you married? What happened?

7. What kind of ministry, if any, does your church have to help women (and men) work through their grief over the

loss of a loved one? Is there any effort made to assist women in their emotional, financial, and emotional transition from marriage to widowhood?

8. What type of behavior between a mother and daughter-in-law might prevent the kind of close relationship which Ruth and Naomi shared? What might contribute to their closeness?

MY SISTER'S KEEPER

Read: Luke 10:38-42 (John 11:1-44; 12:1-8)

My name is Martha. I have been accused by some of being bossy, argumentative, and aggressive. Many say I am a shrew. But what I have been, I have had to be. I am a woman trying to make it in a man's world. There are those who belittle me because the kind of work which I do best, and enjoy doing, is considered worthless in a man's world. But I like cooking, cleaning, mending, washing, marketing, and all the other tasks that go into making our home comfortable for the weary. And I don't mind saying that it takes an inordinate amount of organization, foresight, and stamina to run a household smoothly — more than the average person has, if I must say so myself. And understandably, there are times when the pressures of juggling the demands of shopping, cooking, and cleaning can leave one's nerves on edge.

Imagine Jesus as a guest at your home, and perhaps you will understand why I was so anxious to make sure everything was perfect. Oh, I will admit that my temper got the best of me and I probably spoke too harshly. But imagine what it's like to be saddled unexpectedly with twelve extra mouths to feed! Of course, any woman worth her weight in salt can prepare a meal for four. And four was all I was expecting: the Stranger, Jesus; my brother,

Lazarus; my sister, Mary; and myself. But my brother failed
to mention that wherever the Galilean Stranger went, his
twelve disciples were sure to follow.

I ended up having to figure out how to make a fowl
only large enough to feed six, stretch to feed sixteen. Not
to mention the fact that more cucumbers, beans, lentils,
onions, leeks, vegetable marrow, and garlic had to be
chopped up. As I scurried from pot to pot, from broth to
bread, trying to keep the breeze outside from extinguishing
the fire in the oven, worrying whether there was enough
water and who would go down to the well to fetch more,
I found myself growing increasingly annoyed at my younger
sister, Mary, for leaving me to worry and serve alone. There
was so much to do, so many to do it for, and so little time
to do it. As usual, Mary was engrossed with the conversations of the men. She had even forgotten to offer our travel-
weary guests the opportunity to wash their hands and feet
after a day's journey.

From my cooking area I could see into the front room
where everyone was gathered. The twelve sat in a corner
with my brother, Lazarus, talking among themselves. From
time to time one of them would look jealously over in the
direction of Mary and Jesus. There Mary sat at Jesus' feet,
gazing intently up into his face, looking as though her life
depended on his word, oblivious to the dirt and grime on
his feet. He sat before her speaking with intense urgency,
as though his own life depended on getting out what he
held inside. The two of them, Jesus and my sister, were only
a few feet away from me, but they looked as if they were
miles away from my broth and lentils.

Like I said before, everyone tends to underestimate the
amount of labor and talent it takes to coordinate shopping,
preparing meals, cleaning, tending to ill family members,
and doing it all within a tight household budget. If I'd been
born a man instead of a woman, I could have been one of
the twelve disciples who followed the Galilean and could

have done as good a job — if not better — than any of them in attending to the details of setting up engagements, arranging for meals, securing lodging, and doing the host of other tasks that go into keeping a religious organization running smoothly. At least under my care, Jesus wouldn't have had to sleep in boats and on mountains.

But I was not born a man. I was born a woman. And despite the fact that people only mention my name in the shadow of my sister and brother who are better known than I am, I have done the best I could to carve out a niche for myself. Even if that niche is doing the work — the spade-work of domesticity — that no one else wants to do. But the truth is, I am just one of many women who, because of what we do, keep movements and homes together. I will grant you that I am sometimes a bit tactless and short-tempered. And if this is true, it is because I have found that some people think they can climb on your back anytime they want just because you make your living on your knees.

That's the way my sister, Mary, acts toward me sometimes. People like her think because you're always busy doing housework — every time they see you, your hands are in a batch of dough, or there's soot on your nose, or you smell like onions and garlic — you don't have a mind. Well, I *do* have a mind; and I *do* pray and meditate. Not as much as I'd like, but more than some people think. It's just that women like me have had to learn to talk to God with a broom in our hands. If we don't make the sacrifices that it takes to keep the home going, who's going to do it? Certainly not Mary!

Mary has always had a gift for making people feel important. No matter how boring their conversation, no matter how impractical their assertions, Mary has a gift for making people think they have something valuable to say. She lends them her ears and her heart; she gives them her undivided attention and sympathy. It is a rare gift of con-centration I've never understood.

I, on the other hand, look perpetually distracted. I suppose the only way I know how to express my love and concern is by cleaning and fussing, for I've never known the luxury of self-contemplation. Mary, by contrast, is quiet, sensitive, and at times given to unusual outbursts of affection. Take, for example, the time she stunned everyone by anointing Jesus' feet with expensive oil and then wiping his feet with her hair. Only a slave does such a thing! I was aghast! Yet, admittedly, her sensitivity and humility touched even my heart.

Humility. . .do you suppose that's what I lack? I serve, but without humility. My sister is humble, though she forgets to offer you water.

That afternoon when Jesus was a guest in our home changed my life. And like most worthwhile change, it came about as a result of pain. I had the best of intentions; vexing Jesus was the *last* thing I wanted to do. I had been so anxious that everything go smoothly, anxious that our guests enjoy the meal that I'd been preparing for more than three days, anxious that Jesus be impressed with all that I'd done for him, that I resented the way Mary was consuming his attention with so little effort on her part. It was as if everything I stood for was being held up for public ridicule. Before I knew it, my irritation with my sister got the best of me.

> "Lord, do you not care that my sister has left
> me to serve alone? Tell her then to help me"
> (Luke 10:40).

Silence fell over the room. The disciples looked up from their conversations. My brother, Lazarus, gazed at me in horror. Admittedly, my complaint might have sounded petty and selfish, but in the end, not one of them denied being hungry.

Jesus had only to look up at me with those eyes that seemed to bore right into my private thoughts, and I felt my anger melt to shame. I knew right then that there had never been a time that evening when he had *not* noticed me.

> "Martha, Martha, you are anxious and worked up over many things. But only one thing is important. Mary has chosen the good part which will not be taken from her" (Luke 10:41-42).

Jesus' rebuff stung me, and the look of disappointment on his face sent a chill down my spine.

It was not that he did not appreciate the effort and care that went into coordinating a meal, or the added burden of preparing for unexpected guests. He understood my frustration. No, it was not my housework that Jesus took exception to; it was my attitude. There is a difference between serving and ministering.

I now understand what the Master was saying to me. I know also what he was *not* saying. Jesus was not denigrating the value of my work over against Mary's attentiveness. But in spite of all the sweat and energy that I poured into my service to my guests, my disposition threatened to cancel out all the love that went into my efforts.

And there was more.

My sister and I are different, and there is no way of changing that fact. Nor is there reason to apologize: we are women who have the right to our differences. Nevertheless, we are sisters. And as my sister's sister, I had no right to attack her publicly, certainly not in a room full of men. I should have taken her aside to express my frustrations — woman to woman. And if she had refused to help me, perhaps then I would have had grounds to complain to Jesus.

In truth, my sister has never been interested in housework. Why did I expect that evening to be any different? Who was I angry at? Mary, for not helping me? Jesus, for appearing not to notice me? Or everyone, for expecting me to serve them?

Still, perhaps it was unfair to ask Mary to give what she had no talent for doing. I'm really not sure about that, but I do know I had no right to humiliate my sister before a crowd of people. I wanted to hurt her just as she had hurt me by leaving me alone to serve. In the end both of us were wrong: Mary, for taking me for granted; and I, for not going to her personally to voice my complaint. My Lord, how easy it is for sisters to abuse one another!

My name is Mary. And for as long as I can remember, my sister, Martha, and I have always been different. We look different. We talk differently. We behave differently. We see the world differently. I suppose, we dream different dreams.

But, then, I am different from most of the Jewish women I know in Bethany.

Ever since I was a little girl, I've never wanted to do anything other than read, write, and study. "But such things are not permitted Jewish girls," Mother would say, "so finish peeling your onion." How I would envy my brother, Lazarus, as he'd leave home every morning for his Torah lessons with the local rabbi. How I would envy the way he and Father would stay up evenings arguing the Law, reciting Scripture, and exchanging insights about things that were sealed away as forbidden mysteries to me.

Perhaps if I were more like Martha, it wouldn't hurt so much to have been born female.

My sister has always been quick to speak her mind and the first to take the initiative. She was Father's favorite. . . although one would normally expect such qualities in a girl to have been insufferable to a traditional Jewish male like our father. One thing saved my older sister, despite her impulsive, brash outbursts: my father's oldest daughter was always willing to serve and give herself to others. For this, my father, as most Jewish men would, loved my sister, Martha.

It isn't that I refuse to serve, but that I prefer to listen. I suppose I'm the curious type. By listening in on my father's conversations with the men who dropped by our house to fellowship around fish and wine, I learned about current events: the political intrigues in Herod's court, the disputes between the Pharisees and Sadducees in the Sannhedrin Council, the terrorism of the Zealots, and the death of one John the Baptist. Had I been born male, I would have been a philosopher. But I was born a female. And because I am a woman instead of a man, I am called a daydreamer.

New ideas, exciting discoveries, a lively debate, and other people's conversations — these are the matters that captivate me. Which is probably why my brother invited the Teacher from Galilee to our home that afternoon. Lazarus knew that the love in Martha's heart was in the good she did with her hands, while my heart was in my mind.

I had heard rumors about the thin, dark rabbi from Galilee. Some called him a lunatic. Others thought he was a charlatan. Most believed he suffered from self-delusion. It was rumored that he was a miracle worker, a man of immense power. His was not the political power of King Herod, nor the religious power of the High Priest Caiphas. His was an unusual power that comforted rather than threatened. They said he healed the lame, restored sight to the blind, and gave sanity back to the insane. Even the winds and waves obeyed him, they claimed. Since his frame was slight and his countenance meek, you could easily mistake him for a weak man. But how wrong you would be.

The most persistent rumor of all was that he was a "ladies' man." On many occasions he had been seen talking with women in public. Menstruating women touched him without fear of rebuke. Harlots, adulteresses, and Samaritan women followed him from town to town. Mothers sought him to heal their children, and little girls thought of him as a friend. Such things were unheard of for a respectable Jewish man.

Many people gave everything they had simply to hear him preach. And I know why: when I heard him speak, something inside me fell on its face.

Of course, my brother told me of the wisdom of Jesus' deceptively simple stories: the parable of the prodigal son who returned to the home and family he'd once abandoned (Mark 15:11-32); the shepherd who left his ninety-nine sheep to seek after the one lost sheep (Luke 15:3-7); and the sower whose mustard seed, like the kingdom of God, was the tiniest seed of all, but once planted became the grandest resting place for fowl — and human alike (Luke 13:18-19). All of these stories were enchanting, I agreed.

But these were not the parables Jesus recounted to me when he was a guest in our home. Instead, as I sat at his feet, the Teacher compared God to a woman who loses a coin, searches relentlessly for it, and invites her friends to join her in celebration when she finds it (Luke 15:8-10). He recounted the parable of the poor widow who gave her last coin to the temple (Luke 21:1-4). He told me the parable of the wise and foolish virgins who grew weary with their oil lamps waiting for the bridegroom (Matthew 25:1-4). My favorite of all was the parable about the widow who wouldn't take ''no'' for an answer, even from an impious judge (Luke 18:2-5). To me, Jesus spoke of women, righteousness, and God.

It was as though he was saying to me, ''Mary, the kingdom of God belongs to you, a woman, too.'' It was as though the most important thing to Jesus right then was that I, a woman, understand him. His words held me spellbound.

That was until I heard the sound of my sister's voice. It was a familiar sound, crackling with irritation:

> "Lord, don't you care that my sister has left
> me by myself to serve? Tell her, then, to help
> me" (Luke 10:40).

If I told you I was displeased when I heard Jesus defend my right to learn, I would be less than honest. In fact, I was more than a bit smug. At last I'd met someone who didn't think I was a freak; someone who didn't think my wanting to learn was unfeminine; someone who believed that my curiosity was more than normal, it was commendable.

> "Martha, Martha, you are anxious and
> worked up over many things. But only one
> thing is important. Mary has chosen the
> good part which will not be taken from her"
> (Luke 10:41-42).

Imagine: Centuries of women's intellectual suppression was toppling before my eyes. But the pained expression on my sister's face soon turned my glee to remorse.

Martha was not challenging my right to learn. She was simply challenging my right to do so at her expense.

Nor was Jesus defending my learning at my sister's expense. Actually, it was the way he looked from my sister, standing in the door of the cooking area hurt and embarrassed, to me sitting at his feet uncomfortable and silent, that made me bow my head in shame. It was as though he was waiting for us to talk to one another, rather than talk to him *about* one another.

Yes, my sister, Martha, and I are as different as night is from day. And there are many things about which we don't, and probably never will, agree. But Martha *is* my sister. And she has the right to be supported, too. When I am honest, I have to admit that Martha has always supported me by doing the work around the house which I have always been too preoccupied, too lazy, or too absent-minded to do.

That afternoon in our home as our family entertained Jesus and his twelve disciples, when I did not offer to help my sister in the endless tasks that were before her, I was guilty of exploiting her talents. The truth is, it was because my sister worked as hard as she did shopping, cleaning, and cooking that I was free to lounge undisturbed at the Teacher's feet and contemplate. Never once did I think to ask Martha whether she wanted to join the conversation, or whether there was anything I could do to help her so the two of us could learn together from Jesus.

We women must pool our resources, our gifts, our energies, so that each of us has the opportunity to grow. Sometimes it means making the sacrifice of doing what we are ill-suited to do, like house-cleaning, so that another woman, the one who usually does the house-cleaning, might be free to experience something different.

What good is it if I grow and my sister, Martha, doesn't?

Yes, I might have been justified in my thirst for knowledge. But I was wrong to use my sister to get what I wanted. I should have gone to Martha and offered the few domestic skills I have so that she could have been free to join us. Or, I should have talked the men in the room into doing what I am told they do often — go without food. That way all of us would have been free of the distraction of cooking and serving. All of us could have shared in the learning together.

That is what I *should* have done. How easy it is to think of what we should have done differently, once we've already hurt the ones we love the most. And now, I must go to my sister, Martha, and ask her to forgive me.

Questions for Thought

1. How would you evaluate the relationship between Mary and Martha? Was one sister more at fault than the other? In what ways? Which sister are you most like?

2. Is sibling rivalry inevitable among children? How can parents best respond to and negotiate the jealousy, insecurities, and competitions that arise among siblings for their parents' attention and affections?

3. What are the ways in which you and your own sister(s) are similar? How are you different? How have your differences been helpful in your growth? In what ways do your differences compliment one another?

4. What are your personal values concerning "serving" versus "learning" as seen in the story of Martha and Mary? How/where do the Martha and Mary parts of yourself conflict? Which needs to be developed more within you? Are there situations in which one posture is more suitable?

5. With the influx of women into ordained ministry, how has the role and importance of traditional female leadership and participation in the church (missionaries, deaconesses, stewardesses, etc.) changed? In what ways can women in ordained ministry help and support these traditional organizations? In what ways can the church auxiliaries help support women in the ordained ministry?

6. What role have media played in shaping the image of housework? More specifically, in what ways do commercials

influence and manipulate the consumer habits of women? What are some of the commercials which have played an important role in impacting women's images of themselves? To what extent have the media's portrayals of women shaped your view of yourself?

7. Do you think women should be financially compensated for doing housework, especially those women who do not work outside the home? What kind of remuneration would you propose, if any?

A CRYING SHAME

Read: Judges 11:1-40

WARNING: This story may be deceptive.

After one sober reading, we come to realize that the Old Testament story of Jephthah and his daughter should carry this label.

On the surface, the story is about religious integrity: a man spares nothing to honor a vow he has made to the Lord.

It is a story about radical obedience: a child submits herself dutifully to her father's will.

In a word, it is a story about devotion: a man's devotion to his god and a daughter's devotion to her father.

On the surface, devotion is a very noble concept, one worthy of exploring and expounding. Although, to some, it may sound a bit old-fashioned, it deserves our sincerest reflection. Unlike talk about loyalty and obedience — two concepts often bantered about in political and religious spheres — a discussion of devotion shifts attention away from the devotee to the one who is the *object* of devotion. The focus is no longer on blind submission, as with loyalty and obedience, but on *sacred responsibility*.

But in the story of Jephthah and his daughter, somewhere nobility turns into a nightmare, devotion turns into death. Somewhere the quest for honor and duty, in the face of a young woman's senseless death, becomes a gross distortion of justice.

Jephthah was a brave and gallant fighter. *But.... * In spite of his bravado and gallantry, he was stigmatized among his people.

> "But *he was the son of a harlot"* (Judges 11:1).

Can't you imagine the conversations of his townspeople?

> "Did you know that Jephthah, the young warrior, is illegitimate?"
> "You mean, born out of wedlock?"
> "Yes, a bastard child."
> "Isn't it a shame? Such a fine young man, too."
> "If it weren't for the fact that he's illegitimate, who knows what he could have been."
> "Too bad."

Because of the circumstances of his birth, circumstances beyond his control, a shadow was cast over Jephthah's reputation and future. Jephthah was a skilled warrior, gallant in battle, *but.... * He had grown up in his father's house, but because he was the son of another woman, the son from another union, his half-brothers banished Jephthah from his father's house. In so doing, his brothers cut him off from his share of his father's inheritance. Ashamed and bitter, Jephthah fled and began to use his otherwise admirable talents in a life of crime.

Ambition made Jephthah hungry. When the elders of Gilead enlisted Jephthah's support in a battle against their enemies the Ammonites, Jephthah agreed to help only if they would install him as leader of the Gileadites.

Ambition also made Jephthah impulsive and blind. In his desperate effort to atone the circumstances of his birth, and in his zeal to defeat the Ammonites, Jephthah risked everything he had in order to obtain what he imagined he lacked. He bargained with God.

Ambition caused Jephthah to be so consumed with what he thought he lacked, he lost sight of what he did have.

When ambition is an earnest effort to stretch toward excellence, there is nothing wrong with it *per se.* The problem arises when ambition begins to reach beyond excellence in a grasp for power and prestige. Then, not only can ambition make us impulsive and blind, it can also make us vulnerable. It can seduce us into making promises we cannot keep. It can make us neglect relationships, exploit friendships, and forget vows we made to those dear to us.

In our attempts to secure that which our egos crave, we may risk placing ourselves at the mercy of brutes and those who do not care about us. We may become vulnerable to those who have what we clamor for. And we may become vulnerable to the fear, insecurity, and hunger that drive us to clamor. In short, ambition can make us vulnerable to foolish vows — even vows to God.

Eager to avenge his less-than-honorable birth and to prove himself worthy of the Gileadites' trust, Jephthah struck a bargain with the Lord. If the Lord would grant him victory over his people's chief rival, the Ammonites, Jephthah promised to make a sacrificial offering to the Lord on his return from battle.

> *"If thou will give the Ammonites into my hand, then what/whoever comes forth from the door of my house to meet me when I return in victory from the Ammonites will be the Lord's and I will offer that one up for a burnt offering"* (Judges 11:31).

The foolishness of Jephthah's vow hardly deserves comment. Exactly whom did Jephthah expect to come out of the door to meet him upon his return? If not his daughter, then surely a servant. There is something immediately suspicious about the *recklessness* of this vow.

Following a successful military campaign against the Ammonites, the triumphant warrior returned home where celebration greeted victory. And, as is the case when soldiers of war return home — especially heroes — family and friends came out full of cheer and jubilation to welcome him back. There was nothing unreasonable about Jephthah's daughter dashing out the door of her house that day to greet her father. With timbre and with dance, the unsuspecting young woman ran to welcome home her victorious father.

But joy met sorrow, delight encountered disgust. And, worst of all, acclamation stumbled on accusation. In a perfect example of what is known as blaming the victim, Jephthah lashed out at his only begotten daughter, accusing her of bringing disaster upon him:

> "*Good grief, my daughter! You have surely brought me grief! You have become a pain to me!*" *(Judges 11:33).*

Jephthah projected upon his daughter that which rightfully belonged to himself. Because of *his* thoughtlessness, it was he, Jephthah, who would inflict pain on his daughter. Yet Jephthah talked as though he was the victim when, in fact, it was his unnamed daughter who would become the victim of his foolish vow.

But what did the young daughter feel when she discovered her father's foolish vow? Anger? Rage? Could she have been as compliant and passive as the narrator (presumably male) indicates? If she had argued with her father or resisted his attempt to make her his scapegoat, how different might the outcome of this story have been?

We have a right to ask these questions.

Imagine how the young daughter must have felt!

We have a right to use our imaginations. We must imagine the young woman's immediate reaction. Although it was of no interest to the narrator, her reaction must be of interest to us as women. For, too often, we find ourselves the victims of male righteous reasonings.

What do you do when you discover that someone you love has bartered your life away on account of an impulsive vow?

The young woman's joy gave way to sobriety. She who had come forth with dance and exultation, because of the glory of her father's victory, now stood still, composed and humbled before the gravity of her father's foolish vow. And in one scandalous remark, Jephthah's daughter delivered over to her thoughtless father that which women for centuries have fought to retain: the right to her life.

> *"Do to me according to what has gone forth. . ."* (Judges 11:36).

No fancy intellectual work on the part of theologians, feminists, translators, and preachers can take back what Jephthah's daughter gave up that afternoon. It is an irredeemable remark.

If only the young woman had screamed, kicked, fought, cursed, even fled, anything — absolutely *anything* — but surrender.

As horrible as her surrender was, as much as it offends our sense of righteous rage, we can take courage, however, that Jephthah's daughter did choose *how* she would spend her last days. For that, we can be grateful. She chose to spend her final days in the company of her girlfriends:

> *". . . leave me alone for two months so I may go down to the mountains and lament my virginity, I and my girlfriends"* (Judges 11:37).

As a woman in a culture where women were without voice and autonomy, maybe Jephthah's daughter was powerless to avert what was about to happen to her. But she did show remarkable resolve in her decision to design her own memorial.

Jephthah was probably stunned by his daughter's petition and undoubtedly hurt by her preference to be with her girlfriends instead of himself. He was forced to surrender his daughter to something he could not understand: women sharing one another's grief. "Go," was the most he could bring himself to say to his daughter's strange request.

And so the story goes. For two months the daughter of Jephthah and her girlfriends sojourned together across unnamed mountains, lamenting the daughter's fate and sharing her despair.

There is a sorrow known only to women; a sorrow so profound and so bottomless, it can only be shared with a woman; a sorrow that only another woman can help you bear. It comes from the feeling of having been violated, betrayed, and abandoned by a force much stronger than yourself. And when the force is someone you trusted, the sorrow can be unbearable.

Hence, it should come as no surprise that Jephthah's daughter called her girlfriends together to lament her life. We can thank her for initiating one of the earliest recorded female professions: mourning women.

Mourning became a recognized profession for ancient women (Jeremiah 9:17; Luke 23:28). There was something peculiar in the nature of women, it was believed, that made crying easier for them. As a result, a whole tradition and profession developed whereby women were invited to express in tears and moans what, in a misogynist society, no doubt was too dangerous to express with words.

Mourning women were hired to congregate and lift up appropriate laments in times of death and disaster. They were women who, at a moment's notice, could lift up their voice in a wail and arouse others to respond likewise with sympathy and tears. They were women who could penetrate the heart of even the fool; they could look beyond merriment and see tragedy, beyond tragedy and see death, beyond death and see God.

Prophets, rarely. Scribes, hardly. Priests, never. They were women whose lives were circumscribed within a patriarchal society. But the one profession they were permitted was the one profession they perfected: mourning tragic foolishness.

What might their songs of sorrow have expressed? At least one song would have lamented that it is a crying shame that the redemption story is littered with the bodies of innocent women: daughters sacrificed; martyrs burned at the stake; witches drowned; sorceresses decapitated; preachers banished, whose only crime was being women who saw doors and opened them.

But it would be inaccurate to suggest that only women were privy to the sorrowfulness of human foolishness. Over the years a few men have distinguished themselves as unashamed to weep over sin. Jeremiah was one.

Scattered throughout his prophecy are lamentations and confessions of anguish that have earned him the title of the "weeping prophet" (Jeremiah 9:1,ff.). Whereas other prophets are remembered for the grandeur of their prophecy, Jeremiah is remembered for his inability to hide his feelings. In our society Jeremiah would be considered a "cry baby."

In the not-too-distant past when we were growing up, one of the most painful and damning things that our peers could have called us was a "cry baby." Remember the horrible taunt, "Cry, baby, cry; wipe your weeping eyes"?

Whereas girls were permitted to show their emotions and cry, boys were taught early to stifle their tears. For to cry was to be out of control, emotional, frail, weak, powerless, vulnerable. In a word, feminine. And that would never do.

But thanks to Jeremiah, we have a model of a prophet who was not ashamed to include as part of his memoirs moments of his most painful outbursts before God and his deepest disappointments. And when he became exasperated with the sin before him, when he felt unable to utter another word and plead any further with the people, he was man enough to enlist the support of women to take up where he had failed.

On at least one occasion, Jeremiah called for the mourning and wailing women to come and do what he had failed to accomplish (Jeremiah 9:17). Perhaps the mourning women could bring the people of Judah to their senses.

Is it possible that Jeremiah gained his respect for these professional, weeping mourning women as a result of having witnessed his mother make the annual pilgrimage to mourn Jephthah's daughter, four-hundred-years after her death? Could Jeremiah's mother have been a professional mourner? Could Jeremiah, on one of the many occasions when he had to accompany her as a little boy, have discovered in those gatherings of lamenting women the power that comes from crying and the strength that comes from being able to cry? Perhaps he had observed that, at times, the tears of his mother and the women around her brought change and repentance where prophesy and sacrifice had failed. Perhaps it was in dedication to the memory of his mother and her weeping girlfriends that Jeremiah composed the book of Lamentations. Or, perhaps, the book of Lamentations is an anthology of the laments that Jeremiah's mother and the other women of Judah raised at the destruction of the holy city in 587 B.C.E., laments edited by Jeremiah.

Whatever influenced Jeremiah, we can be grateful that Jephthah's daughter, in her one moment of resolve, found a ministry for women to women: the ministry of weeping with God.

But more than a young woman's virginity was lamented out there on those mountains. The daughter of Jephthah and her girlfriends huddled in a circle and wept over more than children unborn and ecstasy unexperienced. Each of her girlfriends knew that what was about to happen to Jephthah's daughter could happen — without warning — to any one of them.

For every woman who lives in a society which values notions more than it does women lives with the risk of annihilation.

So, the women cried inconsolable tears that day. They wept for Jephthah's daughter. They wept for themselves. And they wept for their daughters' daughters. They knew that the worst lie of all was that, in the end, this would not be the daughter's story, but the father's. So, they wept for a name never known and a whole story that would never be told. And the silent horror of it all would drive them back out to those mountains year after year to cry all over again.

The story of Jephthah's daughter *is* deceptive.

It is deceptive because it is about something graver than honor, integrity, and obedience — for too often noble ideas are corrupted in the hands of extremists and the insane.

As I write this, I am listening to a news report of a North Jersey teen-ager who, after a bitter argument ending in failure to convince his senior high school girlfriend not to have an abortion, doused her family's home with gasoline and set it afire. Not only was the girlfriend killed, but also the fetus he did not want aborted, along with a number of other residents of the dwelling. Who taught this deranged young man that the best way to make a woman obey is to kill her? How did the argument for life and love get equated with a match and torture?

Unfortunately, there are other stories of horror, such as the one of the estranged husband who shot his wife because he didn't believe in divorce; and the elderly husband in Florida who could no longer stand to watch his beloved wife of more than forty years waste away from Alzheimer's disease, so he shot her in the head — *three times*. Somewhere, a love story goes awry. There is something immoral here in the quest for morality.

Someone really ought to call for the mourning women. It's a crying shame.

Jesus found himself confronted with the same flagrant disregard for the lives of women when brutes dragged before him the woman "caught" in adultery (John 8: 3-11). These men, too, were willing to sacrifice a woman for a notion of what is sacred.

They reminded Jesus that the law of Moses commanded that "such" be stoned to death. But before he spoke, Jesus knelt down and wrote something in the dirt with his finger. What he wrote, we are not told. I can hardly forgive the narrator for not taking the time to go over to see. Those words may have saved at least one more of the thousands of women who have been executed over the centuries as a result of some man's misguided notion of what is right.

Just think. It could have saved one more woman.

Someone really ought to call for the mourning women. It's a crying shame.

We all have friends, myself included, who are the victims of domestic violence, from the not-so-casual slap across the face and shove across the room, to a brutal kick and much worse. Mothers. Sisters. Aunts. Cousins. Girlfriends. Neighbors. Women tied to men, husbands, fathers, sons, lovers whose only outlet for venting their frustration and anger — rather than cry — is to lash out at the most vulnerable person around, the women who love them. These women — our mothers, sisters, aunts, cousins, girlfriends, and neighbors — live in a vicious cycle with such men.

"But why do they stay?" we ask in horror.

The reasons are as complex and varied as the men and women involved. Some women remain for the sake of their children, not wanting their children to grow up without a father in the home. Some women stay because they feel they have no other economic options. Some stay because they fear living alone, without a permanent man in their life; and a violent man, they reason, is better than no man. Some stay because they cherish the moment of reconciliation which eventually follows the violence: that fleeting moment of his repentance when he is once again romantic, gentle, childlike, and lovable. Others stay because they are addicted to the violence; it is the only life they know. They all have one thing in common: they do not know that they have a right *not* to be beaten.

Someone really ought to call for the mourning women. It's a crying shame.

It takes a strong woman to leave what she knows — even if it is the love of a violent man — to face what she does not know, to face life alone. My mother did.

Recently while on a plane, I was thumbing through a magazine trying to get my mind off my fear of flying. I came across an article of a Philadelphia man who had butchered and chained several women in the basement of his home on Marshall Street. My first impulse was to turn immediately to the next page and read the entertainment section. I stopped myself. I remembered that I had had this same reaction when I had heard about this incident on a television news report a week earlier. Then, I had shaken my head in horror and gone back to my dinner. This time, I studied the picture of the man and his house, and a snapshot of a victim.

This time I wept.

I wept, not just for the victims, though they were worth weeping over. I wept as well for my own callousness. And when I had dried my eyes, I wrote this poem.

Forgive me,
     Is that your arm over there?
     Is that your leg over here?
     Are those chains around your wrist?
Forgive me,
     I almost didn't notice you
     I almost didn't notice that you'd been mutilated
     I almost didn't notice that you'd been decapitated
     I almost didn't notice that you'd been chained to
          a post all night long
Forgive me,
     I almost didn't notice that you were female, black,
          young, alone, curious, and broke
     Like me.
Forgive me.

     But really dears — before I free your wrist,

     tell me. . . .

How could you be so stupid? How could you be seduced by a Cadillac and a roll of cash. Couldn't you recognize a fool and a demon when you saw one?

     Forgive me.
       Neither did I.
       Why should you?
The recognizing of fools and demons is a dying art.

         Besides, you're not the first to be seduced by fools and demons. Women have been seduced by fools and demons before — and lived to tell it. Your fault is that you were not so lucky.

There are other women in the Bible, besides Jephthah's daughter, who were not as lucky as the woman dragged before Jesus. Other women, whose only crime was to love foolish and dangerous men, are strewn across the pages of salvation history with their mangled bodies and wasted blood: women such as Tamar, who was seduced and raped by her half brother Amnon (II Samuel 13:1-22); the concubine without a name, who was offered to strangers by her husband, a Levite, in order to save his own life and was later butchered by him in a sorry attempt to unite the people of Israel (Judges 19:1-30); and Gomer, wife of the prophet, whose husband threatened to beat and publicly humiliate her into loving him (Hosea 1:1-2:13).

The real tragedy is that the violence each of these women suffered is, in fact, incidental to the point of the story.

Someone really ought to call for the mourning women. It's a crying shame.

It has been said before and deserves to be said again: the stories *of* these women are rarely stories *about* these women. Their mutilation is often a part of a larger story about someone else — namely men.

Tamar's story is, in actuality, a footnote to the story of the conflicts among Kind David's sons as heirs of the kingdom.

The concubine's story is incidental to the story of property rights and tribal unity where all the tribes of Israel gathered together to wage battle against the tribe of Benjamin in their commitment to avenge the Levite's loss of his property, namely his wife.

The threats against Gomer are supposed to be overshadowed by the depth of Hosea's love for Gomer as his disloyal wife.

The story of Jephthah's slaying of his daughter is subsumed under the story of male integrity and religious piety.

Somehow, the story of the female victim never quite gets told.

Yet the sound of these women's screaming voices cannot be silenced. They continue to demand a hearing in the

Church; for now, more than ever, the Church cannot afford to turn its head in silence before the horror of the violence that women continue to endure. Stories of women's bodies — stuffed in car trunks, floating naked in ponds, crowding police stations with black eyes, broken ribs, and busted lips — are popular television plots that bore us instead of enraging us. We have, for all practical purposes, become inured to violence.

Nor can the Church afford to overlook its role in chaining women to bullies, brutes, and beasts in the name of sacred submission and obedience. Yet, before we can issue a credible statement on the problem of violence against women, we, the Church, must first be courageous enough to wrestle with the implacable terror in our own backyards. Violence against women and other forms of domestic violence are symptomatic of a larger epidemic of violence in our culture and world. Murder, terrorism, and war have become regular forms of communication and negotiation.

Someone really ought to call for the mourning women. It's a crying shame.

We can be thankful, however, that the story of the fate of Jephthah's daughter does not end on the note of her death. It ends with the commitment of her girlfriends to keep her memory alive in the hearts and minds of women. Her girlfriends memorialized her in a ritual of mourning.

No doubt, they sang. . .they held hands.

They danced. . .they held hands.

They poured libation. . .they held hands.

They called out her name. . .they held hands.

They prayed. . .they held hands.

And then they wept and wept and wept. . .not out of some morbid fascination with the past, but because of their vision of what the future of women's lives must no longer be. Weeping helped to clarify their vision.

The death of Jephthah's daughter was ritualized in song, dance, and tears year after year. She was remembered by the women in her community as an admission that she was not the first woman to have been treated unjustly. Nor, unfortunately, would she be the last.

Nor were the mourning women the first to cry over injustice. Nor would they be the last.

But their example provides women through the centuries with the sacred opportunity of becoming priestesses of sorrow where they, with God, can lament the foolishness of human sin.

Women mourning women.

Women remembering women.

Such was the girlfriends' way of redeeming the slain woman, giving back to her what it seemed her foolish father had succeeded in taking away: her right to a place in history.

Thus, the story of Jephthah's daughter which began as a story about a man's radical devotion to God ends as a story of women's radical devotion to one another — and to the whole truth. It is a story of women once again taking the only weapon they have — their tears — and craftily cultivating a new song for themselves.

Questions for Thought

1. If you have ever overheard or witnessed your neighbor being assaulted by her husband, what have you done: Called the police? Prayed? Gone over to see whether you could help her? Nothing? What might you do differently now?

2. If you see a friend whom you suspect has been beaten, what would you do: Pretend not to notice and wait for her to bring the subject up? Inquire about her bruises? Slip a note in her pocket or on her desk with the name and number of the local women's shelter, rather than confront her directly?

3. What is the name of the local shelter for abused women in your city? What is the procedure for getting women into the shelter?

4. How many women do you personally know (including yourself) who have been the victims of male violence and brutality (which includes anything from the casual slap to be being mugged; from threats to verbal violence; from being beaten to being raped)?

5. How can your local women's guild, missionary or church auxiliary help to provide aid to women in your church who are the victims of domestic violence?

6. If you have the opportunity to meet with other women, break up into small study groups and assign each group one of the stories in the Bible of women who were victimized by violence:

- Tamar (II Samuel 13:1-22)
- The concubine (Judges 19:1-30)
- Dinah (Genesis 34)
- Gomer (Hosea 2:1-23)
- The adulterous woman (John 8:3-11)

Discuss the following: What is the story of the woman's victimization in the passage? What role does her victimization play within the larger drama? Discuss whether the woman's victimization was "worth" the lesson at issue in the chapter.

7. Take a test: Monitor your TV programming for the next week to see how many programs revolve around the story of violence against women. Even if violence against a woman is not the central plotline, how many programs include this kind of violence to "help" the plot along? Organize your church affiliated women's organization to write the network. Include as many members' names on the petition as possible — both male and female.

IN-LAW, IN LOVE

Read: Numbers 12:1-16 (Exodus 2:1-10)

The Scriptures often invite us to share in the details of the eases and tensions of male bonding. We are well acquainted with the rivalry between the two brothers Jacob and Esau, the battles of David and Saul, the friendship of David and Jonathan, the camaraderie of Elijah and Elisha, and the fraternity of Jesus and his twelve male disciples, to name a few. But we only come to know about relationships between women when their relations impact the lives of primary male characters in the Bible.

To the writer of the book of Numbers, therefore, it probably seemed sufficient to say:

> *"Miriam and Aaron spoke against Moses on account of the Ethiopian woman he married..."* (Numbers 12:1).

Yet in this one line there is a hint — no, a clue — to a story about a relationship between two women. This cryptic observation alludes to serious discord between two women, in this case, sisters-in-law. And even though there is nothing more than this one clue about their conflict, and we are left to envision the details on our own, we can be thankful that the Bible is honest about the friction that often emerges within families.

What fault did Miriam find in her brother's new wife? What role did Moses play in the tension between his wife and sister? Why did Miriam turn against her sister-in-law? What were the signs of their conflict?

While the fate of Moses' Ethiopian bride and the relationship between the sisters-in-law were obviously of no interest to the narrator, for us as women looking for stories of ourselves we can recognize, what has *not* been recorded is as important, if not more so, as what has been told.

We always need to listen for the untold story.

Up until the time of her brother's marriage, Miriam had been satisfied with working behind the scenes. Her unique spirit of praise and gift for song had helped to keep up the hopes of the camp as they made their way from the slave-quarters of Egypt, through the deliverance at the Red Sea, through the uncertainties of the wilderness (Exodus 15:19-21). Miriam was, no doubt, grateful just for the opportunity to be near her brother once again and to share, however unofficially, in his ministry as leader of the Hebrew people.

In a time when a woman's sphere was confined almost exclusively to the family and domestic affairs, Miriam, as Moses' closest female relative, presumably enjoyed her brother's confidences and found herself as an often needed advisor. She most likely experienced a certain amount of visibility as Moses' sister and confidante. In addition to her own talents as a leader, Miriam's relationship to Moses made her an influential woman in the Hebrew camp.

No doubt Miriam was as gifted as her younger brother Moses. Her reputation as a poet and songstress (Exodus 13:21), combined with her anointing as a charismatic leader (Micah 6:4), must have made Miriam a figure to be reckoned with by the Hebrews, especially among the women. In fact, Miriam is one of the few women in the Old Testament whom we come to know for herself — both for her strengths and her weaknesses — and not solely for her role as some boy's mother or some man's wife.*

Noted for her courage and persuasiveness, Miriam played an important role in setting the stage for Israel's sacred history of liberation. At the shore of their deliverance from the Red Sea, where the Lord was made known to the little band of ex-slaves as a Deliverer, she beckoned the other women to join her with timbrel in praise and song and dance:

> "Sing to the Lord, for the Lord has triumphed
> gloriously; the horse and his rider the Lord
> has thrown into the sea" (Exodus 15:21).

It was Miriam whom her younger brother Moses had to thank for saving his life when he was still a baby (Exodus 2:1-10).

When their mother could no longer hide Moses from the Pharaoh's edict to kill all newborn Hebrew sons (Exodus 1:22), it was Miriam who kept diligent watch over the floating basket carrying her brother's endangered life down an aimless river.

When the basket stumbled into the arms of a barren Pharaoh's daughter, it was Miriam who convinced the princess to let a Hebrew slavewoman nurse the hungry, crying child. The unsuspecting princess never knew that the shrewd young girl, who had appeared out of nowhere, was providing the occasion for mother and son to be reunited, by royal decree.

While her brother Moses was being raised as a prince in the house of the Pharaoh among luxury and privilege, Miriam was content to spend her days in her slave quarters,

---

*There are a few other women, such as Deborah and Rahab in the books of Joshua and Judges, and the Hebrew midwives Shiprah and Puah in Exodus, who may be classified along with Miriam as self-sufficient heroines.

knowing that her younger brother was alive, looking forward to the day they would be reunited as sister and brother.

At last, the Hebrews were a free people — thanks to Moses and their God. But something happened to threaten Miriam's favored position: her brother Moses took a wife for himself. To make things worse, the woman he married was an outsider, a foreigner — an Ethiopian woman, to be exact.

How quickly the poet and prophetess of praise and thanksgiving became the instigator of discord and discontent! The same gifts Miriam had once employed to unite the people behind her brother's leadership, she now used to undermine his leadership.

However, since a woman's word alone carried no weight, Miriam could never have hoped to succeed in bringing a case against Moses by herself. She needed the support of a man. This was where their brother Aaron came in. Miriam set out to persuade Aaron to join her in challenging Moses' leadership. To do this, she had to exploit what she knew to be a sore spot between the two brothers.

In Egypt Aaron had worked alongside Moses to secure the freedom of the Hebrews. No doubt Miriam reminded Aaron that he, too, had been instrumental in the people's liberation (Exodus 4:10-17). Had he not stood before the Pharaoh along with Moses? Had he not been spokesman when Moses could only stammer? Had he not kept guard over Israel while Moses conferred with the Lord?

Yet, she observed, Aaron had been completely overshadowed by their younger brother Moses. . .even though Aaron had always been more articulate. And of course, Miriam pointed out, she had more foresight than both. It followed, she reasoned to Aaron, that the two of them were as much leaders as Moses:

> "Is it through Moses only that the Lord has spoken? Has he not spoken also through the two of us?" (Numbers 12:2).

As Miriam and Aaron were soon to discover, however, the difference between their leadership and Moses' lay in the fact that Moses had been appointed by God to be the leader of the Hebrew people (Numbers 12:9-16). And that difference made all the difference in the world.

Just think: If Miriam was daring enough to challenge her beloved brother's sacred leadership — Moses, appointed and acknowledged leader of the Hebrews; Moses, insulated from any attack Miriam (or anyone else, for that matter) might have launched against him — there is no limit to what her conduct toward her sister-in-law must have been.

In the end God came to the defense of Moses. But Moses' new wife was not so lucky. Like most wives of public figures, she was an easy target and was left to fend for herself. In all fairness to Miriam — and we do want to be fair — Miriam might have had good reason to be concerned about her brother's marriage. After all, his marriage to a foreign woman might be interpreted by some as a compromise in his loyalty to his own people. His new wife was not a Hebrew: she was a Cushite, an Ethiopian and, therefore, an African.

Perhaps Miriam feared that, in some people's minds, Moses' new wife would be viewed as somehow being related to the very people from whom the Lord had set the Hebrews free.

Perhaps Miriam, as both a prophetess and a devoted sister, simply wanted to protect her brother from the kind of malicious gossip and suspicion that was sure to spread through the camp once word got out that Moses had married a neighbor of their former slavemasters.

Perhaps Miriam's concerns were justified.

Nevertheless, even if Moses' marriage were a grave mistake, it was not the public crime Miriam made it out to be.

To be sure, Moses was a prominent charismatic leader, meaning that any woman he married would naturally become the unwitting candidate for a certain amount of suspicion, even animosity and gossip. The fact that she was a foreigner did not help her. Moses' wife was a stranger, strange to the customs and ways of Moses' people, strange to their god.

But the new woman in the camp was more than an outsider; for Miriam, she was a threat. The Ethiopian woman threatened Miriam's position among her own people. Unlike the former days when Miriam could go in and out of Moses' tent to confer whenever she needed, get his attention and whisper in his ear whenever she wanted, her younger brother was not as accessible to Miriam as he once had been. The confidences that sister and brother had once shared became the privileges of his new wife.

Consequently, Miriam's influence and visibility suffered. She no longer accompanied Moses to public functions, nor spoke on his behalf on special occasions. As a result, she could not command the people's attention as she once had on the grounds that she was the female half of Moses. There was a new woman in her brother's life.

Miriam resented her sister-in-law. She remembered how she had given unselfishly to her brother's ministry; how, in fact, since she was a young girl and he a crying baby, she had made a career of working on his behalf and in his shadow.

It wasn't fair.

She had subordinated her talents, sublimated her gifts, and re-fashioned her dreams in order to build and support Moses' ministry.

It wasn't fair!

This was the thanks she got. All her years of sacrifice and hard work were about to be completely eclipsed by a woman who, Miriam felt, was unsuitable for her brother.

Hurt, frustrated, insecure, envious, and feeling displaced, Miriam set out to make life for her Ethiopian sister-in-law miserable. She knew she could depend upon her kinswomen for their support. Propelled by their own envy of any woman lucky enough to marry their celebrated leader, those who had once sang and danced with Miriam at the Red Sea were only too glad to follow her lead in scoffing at the "intruder" in the camp.

Admittedly, the details of this reconstruction of the tension between Miriam and her sister-in-law may be hypothetical. Nevertheless, it remains true that petty jealousies and lack of communication rouse a considerable amount of conflict within families. And admittedly, speaking as a sister-in-law myself, it is not always easy to share a brother with his wife.

While problems with mothers-in-law have become cliché in our culture — such that the media have made meddling mothers-in-law a commercial genre — curiously, the image of the possessive sister-in-law is less common. But the reality of the possessive sister-in-law is far more common than we admit.

When my two brothers married, I was more than a bit curious about the women they married. Beyond curious, I was downright resentful. Not resentful enough, however, to intrude into their marriages — after all, I lived a thousand miles away, fortunately. But resentful enough to query my sister on the phone unceasingly about what kind of people these women impressed her as being. My sister was not unbiased in her observations: she was as jealous as I. Neither of us knew what to make of these women who appeared to have some mysterious hold on our brothers.

So, during my visits home, my sister and I consoled ourselves by tallying up in our minds our sisters-in-law's shortcomings: one couldn't cook very well and was far too skinny; the other talked and smoked too much. We asked ourselves, rather self-righteously, whatever did our brothers see in these women. As far as we were concerned, "they" (meaning our brothers' wives) were intruders upon some unspoken though important bond between our brothers and us.

What we could not bring ourselves to admit, however — either outwardly to each other or inwardly to ourselves — was that, for the first time since we'd known them, our brothers were content. . .strangely content.

Brothers who were once attentive, accessible, thoughtful, and dependent upon us (or so we thought), married ''them'' and became inattentive, inaccessible, negligent, and less dependent on us. And while we were more than happy to have another woman take on the responsibilities of caring physically for our brothers — God knows we were tired of picking up after them and loaning them money — we were not as happy to share their affections with other women. (I like to think there is an equivalent sort of resentment toward brothers-in-law; but I doubt it). And, yet, the truth is that we had not been especially close as siblings.

So, if we were not especially close, why did my sister and I secretly resent our sisters-in-law? The answer begins with the obvious fact that a new sister-in-law is a stranger. She is one more personality to factor into an already complex and delicate balance of personalities, intimacies, and needs known as the family. In a covenant relationship that is already strained to its limit, her presence is one more personality that has to be taken into account.

There may be a less obvious reason why resentment arises among sisters-in-law, a reason rarely considered. Thinking back on it, the reason for my immediate resentment of my sisters-in-law was my deep resentment over sharing my brothers' affections.

Good male love is so rare. Love from the men in our families — our brothers, fathers, grandfathers, sons, nephews, and uncles — is the only love for which we as women do not have to compete. It is unrequited love in its purest form.

We don't have to earn our father's love.

We don't have to seduce our brothers into loving us.

We don't have to cajole our grandfathers into loving us.

We don't have to enchant our grandsons, court our uncles, or scheme or dress up for our sons' love.

And, for better or for worse, women cherish the love of men, be it the love of the men in our families or that of our lovers — though differently, of course.

And because we are trained to believe that we must compete to earn men's love, a sister-in-law becomes one more woman we have to vie with for a man's affection, or so we think. In so doing, we act as though men, unlike women, are incapable of loving more than one woman at a time, incapable of loving both his mother and his wife, both his wife and his sister, both his mother and mother-in-law, both his daughter and his wife.

Perhaps this is why it is easy to envision a sister-in-law as an intruder, outsider — a foreigner, no less. Instead of seeing her as an ally, or loving her because she is loved by the brother whom we love, we become immediate adversaries.

The same applies to us as wives: we are often envious of our husband's love for his mother, sister, aunt, and others. Whereas we had to earn his love and are anxious about retaining his love, his mother, sister, aunt are loved without conditions. It seems so unfair — on both sides.

After all these years, I like to think that my sister and I have changed our views about our sisters-in-law. Enough tragedy and disappointment have struck our family — the kind of misfortune which called for us to lay down our swords to plan funerals together, piece dreams back together, dry one another's eyes, and hold each other's hand — to witness bridges built where polite walls once stood.

More importantly, I like to think that my sisters-in-law have noticed the change. Now my sister and I wonder why such great women married our brothers.

* * *

In the case of Miriam, her envy and insecurity blinded her to the possibility that in her Cushite sister-in-law she might have found a friend, not an enemy. Had she taken the time to cultivate a relationship, instead of conspiring against her sister-in-law, Miriam might have found her brother's wife to be an advocate on her behalf before Moses. The new bride could have appealed to Moses in ways that, as his sister, Miriam could never have hoped to initiate.

Furthermore, Miriam could have found in her sister-in-law a much needed female friend and confidante with whom she could have shared the hardships and demands of public life and responsibilities. When Moses married the woman from Cush, Miriam was not losing a brother but gaining a potential ally.

But Miriam's jealousy distorted her view. What could have been a story about women pooling their resources, sharing power, forging alliances, and building bridges among themselves, became instead a story about women within the same family allowing jealousy to blind them, insecurity to alienate them.

It is a story all too familiar for many of us.

But the story need not end here.

According to the biblical story, God's anger was provoked by Aaron and Miriam's conspiracy (Numbers 12:9). For her part in arousing discord in the camp, Miriam was struck with leprosy. Not surprisingly, it was her brother Moses' intercession on her behalf before God that resulted in Miriam's healing. For life is often like that: the victim often has to come to the rescue of the victimizer. Which suggests that Moses' wife — the other victim in this story whom the narrator ignores — also may have intervened on behalf of Miriam.

Perhaps Moses' wife convinced her husband to intercede on his sister's behalf.

Perhaps she convinced her husband and the rest of the camp not to set out on their march without Miriam who was quarantined seven days in the wilderness (Numbers 12:15).

Perhaps, in spite of Miriam's malice against her, Moses' wife prayed to God on her sister-in-law's behalf.

We will never know.

But one thing we do know. In order to mend the discord and heal the wounds that issue from the skirmishes that frequently occur within families, especially, and among women in particular, someone has to be willing to take the first step. Even if that first step goes unrecorded.

Questions for Thought

1. Think about your own affections and relationships with your brothers (and sons). Recall your feelings about the women they dated over the years and the women they eventually married. Be honest. Were there ever times when you were envious of the women in your brothers' (or sons') lives? In what ways were your feelings expressed in your relationships with your sisters-in-law (or daughters-in-law)?

2. How has the leadership role of women in the church changed over the last twenty years? Are those changes positive or negative? Evaluate the positive and negative ways in which the Women's Movement in the larger society has affected Christian women's views of themselves and their understanding of the Bible.

3. As black Christian women, what are our responsibilities to the Miriams — the talented but frustrated women — who are members of our boards, circles, and societies. Remember: For all her faults, Miriam was a talented and gifted woman.

4. What are some of the ways in which people in positions of power and/or influence in the church can, and sometimes do, exploit their power and influence in order to manipulate public opinion and undermine leadership? How can we prevent this?

5. As the sister of the leader of the Hebrews, was Miriam's auxiliary relationship to Moses a good one? Do you think

her gifts were being used in the best possible way in that role and relationship?

6. When power is concentrated in the hands of a few members of a church, or in a particular family within a church, consider the impact this has on the life and ministry of the church.

7. What other lessons can family members learn from the story of discord between Miriam and Aaron, on the one hand, and their brother Moses and his wife, on the other?

8. Moses' intervention on his sister's behalf raises the issue of the importance of intercessory prayer within families. What experiences have you had with the effectiveness of intercessory prayer in healing a family conflict?

CERTAIN WOMEN

Read: Luke 8:1-3 (Matthew 27:55-28:10;
Mark 15:40-41, 16:1-13; Luke 24:1-11; John 20:1-18)

Of their call, we have no record. We do not always know where they were born, nor do we know what happened to them after he was gone. Painful as it is to admit, we do not even know some of their names. Yet we do know that an untold number of women followed Jesus — even at the risk of anonymity and of being misunderstood.

Perhaps embarrassed that he could not remember all their names, Luke, the writer of the third Gospel, refers to them simply as "certain women" in the King James translation of the Bible, a designation which calls attention more to their novelty than to their integrity. But at the same time, such a phrase acknowledges — unwittingly, perhaps — that the women's presence was undeniable.

Many of the women attracted to Jesus' radical teaching, according to Luke, were wealthy women: Mary Magdalene, Joanna, and Susanna financed Jesus' ministry out of their abundant resources (Luke 8:1-3); Lydia, a successful businesswoman who specialized in purple dyes, opened her home to the nascent Church (Acts 16:12-15); and more than "a few leading women" of Thessalonica were converted under Paul and Silas' teachings (Acts 17:4). In today's jargon, Mary, Joanna, Susanna, Lydia, and the women of Thessalonica would be called "women of independent means."

But is Luke trying to suggest that only (or particularly) idle, upper-class women were drawn to support Jesus' radical vision? Are we to understand that Jesus called poor men to follow him, but attracted wealthy women as his financial backers? Although we have no reason to doubt the overall accuracy of Luke's Gospel, undoubtedly women from all economic backgrounds — the wealthy, the comfortable, the modest, the poor, and the homeless — were changed by Jesus' ministry. After all, the New Testament is full of stories of women, like Jesus' own mother, who were too poor to find a decent place to give birth (Luke 2:7); like the widow from Nain who, upon the death of her only son, was left destitute and alone (Luke 7:11-17).

And if our own experience as contemporary women in the Church has any validity in helping us envision the kinds of women who followed Jesus, those whom Luke imagined to be financially wealthy women may very well have simply been *committed* women giving all they had to a vision of a new kingdom and a new way of living. Dedicated women are certainly the women who have been the financial spinal column of the black Church — not rich women but generous women, women who give all they have, even when what they have is just a little.

You can find generous, sacrificing women in all churches.

It has not always been the woman with a lot to give who has been the best supporter of the Church; instead, the one who consistently gives what she has is often the one who makes a difference in the Church's survival.

Jesus was well acquainted with such women:

> *"He looked up and saw the rich putting their gifts into the treasury; and he saw a poor widow put in two copper coins. And he said, 'Truly I tell you, this poor widow has put in more than all of them; for they all*

*contributed out of their abundance, but she
out of her poverty put in all the living that
she had'" (Luke 21:1-4).*

The widow gave not a lot, but all she had. And it is
because of the sacrifices of such committed women that
the ministry of Jesus, the ministry of the Church, has
flourished.

So the women whom Luke so fondly speaks of as part
of Jesus' company — whose presence Luke justifies as Jesus'
wealthy financial backers — need not be remembered as
simply idle, wealthy women. As their contemporary sisters,
we should try to see them the way in which they, no doubt,
would have preferred to be remembered.

Mary Magdalene, Joanna, Susanna, and other female
traveling evangelists made up the band of female workers
who surrendered and sacrificed everything to follow Jesus.
Along with the disciples, they, too, traveled with Jesus. But
between teaching, they did the cooking; beyond the recruit-
ing, they did the mending; in excess of donating their funds,
they donated their time. Judging by the disciples' reactions
to Jesus' penchant for stopping to talk with the strange
women who followed him, these women were undeniably
an annoyance to the faithful male followers.

We get a hint of this from the description of the
disciples' amazement that Jesus openly chatted with a
woman in the middle of the day, a Samaritan woman no
less (John 4:7-30); and their utter horror that he permitted
a woman who was a sinner to touch and anoint him (Luke
7:37-50). In those days there were strict religious laws among
the Jews against social intermingling between the sexes.

Have you ever noticed that most often, whenever the
Gospel writers refer to Jesus' female companions, more than
one woman is mentioned? We hear of Mary Magdalene,
Joanna, and Susanna following Jesus from village to village
as he preached the Gospel (Luke 8:1). Luke later tells us

that it was Mary Magdalene, Joanna, and Mary the mother of James who made the daring trek out to the tomb that Sunday morning to claim Jesus' dead body (Luke 24:10). And John writes that three women — Mary, Jesus' mother; Mary, the wife of Clopas; and Mary Magdalene — stood at the foot of the cross, helpless, but committed to the end (John 19:25).

Admittedly, the numbers of women mentioned in the Gospels are not many, but there is always more than one: enough to force the writers and the disciples to take note. One woman can be explained away. One woman among twelve men can be dismissed as "unusual," "different from most women," "more than a woman," or with other silly comments often used to keep one woman conceited about herself, and women as a whole divided among themselves.

Whereas one woman can be overlooked, several women cannot be ignored.

The women disciples knew this, even if Matthew, Mark, Luke, and John did not. Perhaps this is why the women always traveled together, thereby forcing history to remember them as a group, as "sisters." They stayed together because there is strength and visibility when women band together. They were a community of women among an outfit of men, not apologetic for their numbers, but empowered by their shared vision.

One of the women was called Mary Magdalene. Her surname was taken from the place where she was born: the bustling, prosperous shipping district of Magdala, on the Sea of Galilee. Because her name is often the first name mentioned in the lists of women's names in the Gospels, we can assume Mary Magdalene was a leader — if only among the women. At the same time, because there are no less than seven Marys in the Gospels, over the years Mary Magdalene has often been confused with and mistaken for the profiles and sins of many other women.

Although many people have supposed that the sinner who anointed Jesus' feet with her hair and tears (Luke 7) was Mary Magdalene, we have no reason to believe that the anointer and Mary Magdalene are the same woman. Mary Magdalene is not introduced by name until the next chapter, where all we are told specifically about her is that, before she met Jesus, she had been plagued with demons (Luke 8:2).

In those days people believed in spiritual beings, both good ones and bad ones. Those which proffered goodwill were considered angels, and those which proffered evil, demons. As such, mental disorders were believed to be manifestations of demonic spirits.

In Mary, it is told, there were seven demons to be exact.

We do not know the specific nature of Mary Magdalene's illness; however, we do know that once she was healed, Mary proved to be an able leader among the women: articulate, loyal, and persuasive. And because, once she was healed, she was so charismatic, it is not far-fetched to suppose that at least some of Mary's illness was brought on by her inability to express herself fully. That could be attributed to the lifestyle she was forced to live because she was a woman in first-century Palestine.

Imagine: Here was an otherwise gifted, intelligent, bright, charismatic woman living in a society which had no place for gifted, intelligent, bright, charismatic women. Like many women today, Mary's emotional and physical infirmities were probably symptomatic of the stresses she was forced to live through on a daily basis: stresses and strains that came in the form of relationships and environments that were neither affirming nor encouraging; stresses that were, in fact, repressive and destructive.

When we live under circumstances and within relationships that are hostile to our talents, we find our contributions ignored, our possibilities limited, and our dreams under constant attack. We can only imagine what life must have been like for a gifted woman in the first century. No wonder Mary was labeled by the physician Luke as one possessed with "evil spirits and infirmities." Indeed, the "demons" that claimed Mary are the same demons that prey on many of us: depression, fear, low self-esteem, doubts, procrastination, bitterness, and self-pity.

Seven demons. Count them.

These "demons" comprise the profile of every woman who finds herself in circumstances — whether family, career, or church — which prevent her from reaching for, stretching toward, and developing into the woman God intends of her. Unchecked, these "demons" lead to self-destruction. And in light of the pressures many of us face as women in America, especially those of us who are racial ethnic women — trying to juggle the inordinate demands of families and jobs, navigating through reeling and sometimes disintegrating relationships with husbands and lovers, negotiating our needs with those of others who depend upon us emotionally and physically — the truth is that most of us are often only a demon away from depression, two demons away from insanity, and three demons away from suicide.

What did Jesus say to Mary Magdalene one day that gave her back her mind? What did he say that convinced Mary to abandon her demons and join this itinerant band of women and men who were looking for a new way of living and being? Was she in the crowd that evening when Jesus stood near a mountain extending the invitation to discipleship with the words, "Come unto me all who are heavy laden and I will give you rest. . ." (Matthew 11:28)? Perhaps Mary overheard the words intended for the menstruating woman, "Woman, your faith has made you whole" (Luke 8:48), and caught a glimpse of her own healing as well. Whatever it was that Mary heard, one thing is for sure: Mary Magdalene was never the same again.

There were other women who followed Jesus, women like Joanna. All that we know about her is that she was "Joanna, the wife of Chuza, Herod's steward" (Luke 8:2). Which means that we do not know Joanna for who she was as a person, but for who she was as the wife of a high-ranking official in Herod's cabinet. Which probably also means that, before she met Jesus, all of who Joanna was — her name, economic wealth, political clout, and social standing — had been defined through her marriage to Chuza, her husband. These were Joanna's demons: the demons of having no identity separate from one's husband's, no distinction apart from what one owns in life.

But Jesus gave Joanna's life meaning and direction beyond her husband's reputation. What might Jesus have said to her that changed her life? Perhaps it was his sermon on material things: "Is not life more than food and the body more than clothing...?" (Matthew 6:25). Whatever it was, Joanna was free to make a name for herself. She was no longer simply Joanna, the wife of Chuza. She was Joanna, the woman who had done the unheard of: she had combined her marriage with her ministry.

The reference to Joanna as the wife of Chuza, moreover, says something very important to the women's issue of negotiating the demands of marriage and ministry. Some scholars have assumed that Joanna left her marriage to Chuza to follow Jesus. But this need not have been so. There is another way of "explaining" Joanna's presence as a married woman traveling among men.

No one automatically presumes that Peter abandoned his marriage to follow Jesus. Peter, we believe, was simply an itinerant minister who had to leave his wife and family for extended periods of time for his itinerant ministry. The story of his mother-in-law's healing (Luke 4:38-39) suggests that Peter's marriage had not been dissolved.

Why couldn't the same be true for Joanna? After all, Jesus did not come to deny her love, but to assure that her life was more abundant. Could it be that Joanna and Chuza's marriage is a biblical example of the dual career marriage where, in this case, the wife's career required her to be on the road for long periods of time? (Admittedly, this would have been a very unusual marriage according to Jewish standards, but we have no evidence to suggest the contrary.)

Then there was the woman named Susanna. Unfortunately, we know nothing about her. Where was she from? Who was her family? What was her need? Which were her demons? Like so many women, both past and present, Susanna symbolizes the untold number of anonymous women who follow Jesus; women whom we will never know by name; women who, like so many of us, join together, do what has to be done and die.

No one bothers to remember our names. No one thinks it necessary to record our stories. If they remember our first names, then they forget our last names.

Take, for example, Elizabeth, the first recorded African woman to be brought to American shores as a slave in 1619. Was "Elizabeth" her African name? Hardly. Or did she convert to Christianity on the long journey from her homeland and chose for herself "Elizabeth" as her Christian name? Her full name, we will never know.

But her presence is undeniable. More than twenty-five million Americans of African descent are here to prove that indeed "Elizabeth" stepped on these shores.

Likewise, whether we have the honor of knowing their names or not, the presence of the "certain women" who followed Jesus cannot be denied. The disciples, try though they might, simply could not deny their contribution.

Although Jesus called twelve men to be his disciples, it was an untold number of women who followed him to the bitter end. The sight of his body dangling from a bloody cross sent the men scurrying back to the safety and familiarity of their fishing nets, hiding in closed quarters, seeking the protection of anonymity, renouncing the memories they had shared with him.

The women, however — Mary Magdalene, Joanna, Susanna, Salome, Mary the mother of Jesus, and "certain other women" who knew only too well what it was like to be rejected, renounced, condemned, and scoffed at — stood at the cross where Jesus hung, huddled in a circle, leaning and crying on each other's shoulders.

From this circle of women, Jesus, as he had done so often in the past, must have drawn some strength in his final hour. These were the same women who had encouraged him when he was down, affirmed his Messiahship when others doubted, and served him when he was too tired to serve others. And at the cross, they prayed for him when he could not pray for himself.

To his ministry, they had given everything they had: their gifts, talents, time, money. . .their very substance. Anything, to keep his dream going. In short, the women had ministered to Jesus out of the abundance of their hearts.

Unfortunately, none of these first-century female disciples have enjoyed the notoriety accorded their male colleagues. Peter, James, John, Thomas, and the other eight disciples, we know only too well. But the names and stories of the women are barely familiar.

Of the numerous women who came in contact with Jesus as he made his way throughout the land preaching and teaching the good news of the kingdom of God, more often we come to know the women by their sexuality:

> the woman found in an adulterous embrace
> (John 8:1-11);
> the woman with the interminable menstrual flow
> (Luke 8:42-48);
> the woman with five husbands plus one (John 4:7-30);
> the sensual worshiper who, overcome with love,

anointed Jesus' feet with oil and wiped them
with her hair (Luke 7:36-50).

At times, these women had to be demanding (John
2:1-5) to get a hearing by Jesus, and at other times, boisterous
(Luke 11:27-28). At still other times, they had to be stubborn
(Matthew 15:21-28) and insistent (John 20:15). They were
whatever they had to be, because making a name for
themselves in history was not their aim. Freedom and
healing — theirs or that of a loved one — were the aim.

The same holds true in our own history.

Even though she, too, mobilized and led several
hundred black people to freedom, Harriet Tubman's name
has always taken a back seat in history to that of Martin L.
King, Jr.

Ida Wells Barnett, herself a journalist committed to the
thankless task of bringing to public attention the horrors
of Jim and Jane Crow and the lynchings of black men, has
never been granted equal status in the corridors of time with
that of fellow journalist W. E. DuBois.

Had Nannie Helen Burroughs — the former executive
of the Women's Auxiliary of the National Colored Baptist
Convention and a recognized club woman, a woman of com-
manding presence and uncompromising speeches — been
born in another era, she would surely have been a preacher,
if not a prophet. But no one mentions Ms. Burrough's name
along with Adam Clayton Powell, Jr., when they call the
roll of great orators of the twentieth century.

But contributed, these women of African ancestry did.

They marched, spoke, wrote, and fought along with the
best men. The ministry of the Church depended on them,
even when the leadership of the Church ignored them; and
they were forced to go outside the Church to do what needed
to be done within the Church. Like their sisters of anti-
quity — Mary Magdalene, Joanna, Susanna, and the

others — they contented themselves with living on the periphery of authorized ministry, despite the fact that their labors impacted the heart of the movement. The poet Alice Walker refers to such women as "headragged generals."*

As individuals, they have been lost and forgotten in the shuffle of history. But together, they are enduring. Together, as the "certain women" of modern history, they formed for themselves lasting alliances: Stewardess Board #3, The National Council of Negro Women, The Dorcas Missionary Society, Alpha Kappa Alpha Sorority, The Mother Board, and the League for the Protection of Colored Women.**

Fortunately, history writers do not have the final word on the contributions and ministries of women.

The "certain women" of the Bible — like their contemporary sisters who have been ignored, dismissed, spurned, and certainly resented by those responsible for writing history — found support in each other and in the words of their Savior when he reprimanded a male disciple for criticizing one of the women:

> "Truly, I say to you, wherever this gospel is preached in the whole world, what she has done will be told in memory of her" (Matthew 26:13).***

---

*See Alice Walker's poem "Women" in her second collection of poems, *Revolutionary Petunias & Other Poems* (New York: Harcourt Brace Jovanovich, Inc., 1973).

**Organized in 1905, the League for the Protection of Colored Women was founded in New York and later absorbed by the National Urban League.

***There has been a recent spate of efforts by feminist scholars to recover and reconstruct the contributions of women who lived during the biblical era. For one of the most programmatic and noteworthy attempts, see a book by the New Testament scholar Elisabeth Schuessler-Fiorenza, *In Memory of Her: A Feminist Theological Reconstruction of Christian Origins* (New York: Crossroads Press, 1984).

Questions for Thought

1. Are you part of, or do you know of, ways in which Christian women collectively support and finance the work of their local and national church beyond what they might be able to do individually?

2. More and more women are choosing professions which, in the past, have been dominated by men, such as law, construction work, medicine, ministry, aviation, the military, etc. What do you imagine are the disadvantages and advantages of being the "only woman" in a profession or in an office dominated by men?

3. How might the account of Jesus' ministry and teachings been written differently had one of the female disciples written it?

4. What other examples in history can you think of where women's contributions have been overshadowed or ignored, whether in the church or the larger society?

5. How have women's and men's views on marriage changed over the years? Which changes have been positive? What changes still need to take place?

6. In a marriage where one of the partners travels considerably with his or her job, what stresses and strains might the absence place upon the marriage or the family? When the traveling partner is the wife, do the problems become more acute? In what ways can the church help families in these situations?

7. Must a woman choose between a family and a career? Can she be successful at both? What are the tensions for a woman involved in juggling a career and a family?

8. What do you see as the difference between "demon possession" and mental/emotional illness? As Christians, how can we minister to those who suffer from mental and emotional illnesses?

A CROWN OF THORNS

Read: Esther 1:1-2:4

The details and intrigues of Queen Esther's daring reign are so familiar, we almost forget that Queen Esther was not the first queen to defy King Ahasuerus. The standard had already been set by her predecessor, the king's first wife, Queen Vashti. Either King Ahasuerus had notoriously bad luck in choosing wives, or else he was attracted to independent women and didn't know it. His first wife, Queen Vashti, refused to come to the king when summoned; his second wife, Queen Esther, went to the king without summons. The similarity in the two women's defiance is striking.

Here are two women who took advantage of their positions as wives of a prominent public figure to bequeath to us a different image of ancient women, an image suggesting that ancient women were not as passive and resigned to their stations in life as we have been led to believe.

The legend of the two queens Vashti and Esther reminds us of the enormous responsibilities and pressures placed upon women who are married to public figures. It goes without saying that marriage itself is difficult. But to be married to a public figure where one's life becomes a role, and one's relationships susceptible to public scrutiny, can be especially grievous. In the case of Queens Vashti and Esther, each queen was faced with a decision whether to accept or reject the role expected of her. Each woman had to face the consequences of her decision. The outcome of Queen Vashti's story, however, was not as felicitous as Esther's.

A feast had been called in the empire. For his princes, royal subjects, administrative officers, and military personnel, King Ahasuerus (known in ancient history as Xerxes I) threw a big party from Persia to Media. The festivities lasted for more than one hundred eighty days.

Evidently, the king was pleased enough with the mood of the festivities across the land to extend the celebration for seven more days in Susa, the home of his winter palace. The narrator, in what might have been a subtle criticism of the king's self-indulgent tastes and hedonistic appetite, sneaks in a private tour of the palace: windows draped in white cotton curtains with blue borders of fine linen, tied to purple silver rods; marble pillars; couches of gold and silver; and floors made up of a mosaic of precious stones, such as mother-of-pearl and marble.

Unlike the festivities in the other territories of the empire, the banquet in Susa was open to all, the great and small alike. But what is a party without plenty of booze? Drinks were on the house. No one was compelled to drink, but the lavishness of the king's offer — free flowing wine served in golden goblets and other expensive serving ware — must have tempted even the most devoted teetotaler.

Oddly, the big bash taking place throughout the royal city was without cause. It was not to celebrate the king's inauguration, a royal birth, a successful political campaign, or a major military victory. No reason is given for the shindig other than to show off the opulence and splendor of the king's holdings (Esther 1:4). The only way explanation is a big ego trip for King Ahasuerus.

Meanwhile, in a separate quarter of the winter palace, a private party was going on: at Queen Vashti's behest, the women of Susa were enjoying their own ceremonies (Esther 1:9). Had the narrator not been so explicit, we would never have known that the lavish feast in the palace courts was for men only; we would not have known that women were excluded from such public festivities.

Had it not been for Queen Vashti, the women of Susa never would have had an opportunity to join in the festive spirit that filled their land. But, judging by the fleeting mention of the women's gathering, there is some doubt whether the women's party matched the extravagance of the men's. Whether the modesty of the women's celebration was the queen's decision, or whether it reflected the state's attitude toward women's gatherings, it is not certain. Regardless, it is certain that the women of Susa had Queen Vashti to thank for the party they did have.

Surrounded by scores of women from throughout the land — the wives of noblemen and the wives of peasants, many of whom had never witnessed such luxury and wealth and looked to the queen for their cues as how to conduct themselves amidst splendor — no doubt Queen Vashti's every gesture and comment was being observed by the women in the room.

Had the queen been another kind of woman, she could have turned the party for the women of Susa into a worship service for herself. She, like her husband, could very well have used this occasion to showcase her own royal holdings and flaunt her privilege and power over the women of Susa. But in the fleeting mention of the party given for the women, we sense that Queen Vashti took seriously her responsibilities to the women of the land.

Back in the courtyard, however, the mood of the men's party had become lusty. Singing and laughter had reached a feverish pitch. Private dancers and shameless frolic had been exhausted. Those who had not passed out from sheer delight began to do what intoxicated men do best: boast about women they have known. They reminisced about their first loves, their lost loves, and their secret loves. The less delirious compared notes.

Leading the pack was King Ahasuerus. All other women, he waged, paled in comparison to his wife, Queen Vashti. To prove his point, the king dispatched seven trusted eunuchs to bring the queen to him immediately, adorned with her royal crown.

What followed sent shockwaves throughout the kingdom. It was enough to sober the king:

> "But Queen Vashti refused to come as the king commanded..." (Esther 1:12).

Imagine the king's humiliation! Flanked by his drinking buddies on every side — those who made a career of serving the king and obeying him, those who deferred to him in public but plotted against him behind closed doors, and those who were just there for the free wine and a good wager — the king could not afford to tolerate public insubordination, especially from a woman. Even if that woman was the queen.

Perhaps under different circumstances — in the privacy of their chambers or in a private discussion between the two of them over dinner — King Ahasuerus might have been willing to countenance his wife's defiance. Perhaps.

But in front of the men who now looked on in horror, the king had to act and to act quickly. At all costs, it could never be said that the king was hen-pecked. After all, if a man could not rule his own house — which meant his wife and children — then, surely he could not rule a whole empire.

In other words, the king's honor and ego were at stake. The private differences between a man and his wife — a man who happened to be the king and a woman who happened to be the queen of the land — became a public battleground with political and social consequences.

King Ahasuerus called in the wisest men of the land for deliberations (Esther 1:13). Whatever their recommendations, he would follow. The objective was clear: an example would have to be made of Queen Vashti. Too many women looked up to her. If word ever circulated that the king's wife had openly defied the king's orders, anarchy would spread throughout the land.

Women would get all kinds of crazy notions in their heads. They might even get the idea that they were men's equals, capable of making their own decisions, or some such foolishness. No man would be safe in his own house.

In the minds of the men who convened to judge her, Queen Vashti's "disobedience" had social, political, and economic ramifications. Indeed, her behavior posed a threat to the created order, not to mention national security.

For her refusal to leave her female guests and come to her husband when he beckoned, Vashti paid dearly. The rest of the story, we know all too well. In the end, she lost her crown and was, presumably, banished from Susa.

The story of Vashti's reign stands as a valuable lesson about the enormous pressures, demands, and responsibilities upon women who live public lives. It is a memorial to the price often extracted of public women when they step outside of their prescribed roles.

Nancy Reagan, Rosalynn Carter, Eleanor Roosevelt — wives of modern American presidents — come to mind.

There is always a certain amount of meaningless pomp and circumstance that wives of public figures must endure out of courtesy and custom — things such as standing in receiving lines shaking hands with friends, foes, and perfect strangers; accompanying him to banquets to hear him recite the same speech for the fourth time in one week; serving as hostess for endless social gatherings; and smiling through insults and hurting feet.

As wearisome as most of these kinds of "duties" may be, however — and they do eventually take their toll on

one's body and spirit — they are not necessarily demean-
ing, not like the request King Ahasuerus made. His demand
was for his wife to come and display herself before his
drunken guests.

There comes a time when even a queen has to put her
royal foot down and say, "Enough is Enough."

Responding to such a debasing request would not have
served the public interest and, evidently, would have
violated the queen's sense of propriety. Just as the king's
honor depended on his wife's unswerving obedience,
Queen Vashti's integrity, before the company of women who
looked upon her as a role model, depended on her courage
to refuse to compromise. The queen made her decision.

Let us not fool ourselves. The Old Testament story does
not suggest that Queen Vashti was unhappy being a queen,
nor that she was unappreciative of the privileges which
came with being a queen, nor that she despised her
husband, despite his shortcomings. In the times in which
she lived, Vashti, no doubt, was well aware that it was more
prudent to be married than unmarried, more comfortable
to be a queen than a peasant.

But Vashti's story is not simply a recounting of one of
many instances in a marriage where one spouse acts insen-
sitively toward the other, or where one inconveniences the
other. Something more was at stake in the king's request than
the queen's personal comfort. Queen Vashti found nothing
flattering in her husband's desire to show off her beauty
before his drunken guests. She refused, even in the face of
banishment, to comply with his dehumanizing command.

Many women over the decades have followed Queen
Vashti's example of choosing exile over compromise.

Margaret Mitchell, the wife of a former U.S. Attorney
General, comes to mind.

The story of Queen Vashti speaks particularly to the
demands placed upon women married to men in positions
of public leadership. In cultures and institutions where the

role of women has, by and large, been restricted to the domestic sphere; where the participation of women in decision-making has been severely limited; in these settings, what little leadership experience many women have garnered has come as a result of their roles as wives of public figures: wives of politicians, civil rights activists, ministers, actors, entertainers, and other men who have distinguished themselves. In the case of the black and other minority communities, much of our enduring female leadership has come from the Church, particularly from the minister's wife.

For those of us raised during the age of twentieth-century feminism — where we have witnessed and been the beneficiaries of significant social, political, and economic gains made by women in both the public and private sector — it may appear somewhat old-fashioned, if not downright counterproductive, to talk about women whose status and position are a function of their roles as wives of public men, women whose power and influence are derived from their relationships with men.

Like Queen Vashti, the circumference of the power of these women has often been confined to issues that concern women. But many times in the past — and it continues often to be the case even in the present — it is precisely because of their relationships and access to certain kinds of information that these women have been able to monitor and act as advocates for policies and issues that immediately impact women. Their marriages have often provided them with the opportunities to act and speak on behalf of women in corridors often closed to women's interests.

Some of the women who have made the greatest contributions in our history have been wives of public figures. Sometimes they have exceeded their husbands in talent; many times they have continued the work begun by their husbands; other times they have surpassed their husbands in popularity.

Many women come to mind:

> Corazon Aquino, wife of slain activist Benigno
> Aquino;
> Jihan Sadat, wife of the slain Egyptian head of state
> Answar Sadat;
> Shirley DuBois, wife of spokesman W. E. B.
> DuBois;
> Eleanor Roosevelt, wife of former president
> Franklin D. Roosevelt;
> Coretta Scott King, wife of the slain civil rights
> leader M. L. King, Jr.;
> Winnie Mandela, wife of jailed South African
> political activist Nelson Mandela;
> Betty Shabazz, wife of slain Muslim activist
> Malcolm X;

The wives of ministers also come to mind — especially for those of us in the black community. The role that the black Church has played in the history of black people in America can never be overstated. Under the leadership of its ministers and their wives, the black Church has been the most enduring institution of political, economic, and social activism on behalf of black Americans. Therefore, like their husbands, women such as Coretta Scott King, Jacqueline Jackson (wife of the Rev. Jesse Jackson), and countless others have found themselves called upon to do everything from chairing local and national fundraisers for black colleges and coordinating local church activities, to acting as mistress of ceremonies at fashion shows and serving as a national speaker on assorted topics related to women, children, and the handicapped. Their contributions are innumerable.

Like their predecessor Queen Vashti, these women's marriages have provided them with opportunities not only to make use of their immense talents, but also to monitor closely the local and national issues which concern them.

Moreover, their marriages to men in positions of public leadership have given them immediate access to the lives of hundreds of women, whereby they could mobilize women across the land into political, social, and moral actions.

But the story of Queen Vashti shows us that, depending upon the temperament of the woman involved, some demands placed on a wife of a public figure can be viewed as either an intrusion upon her privacy or a challenge to her talents. Even the wives of public figures have their own temperaments and talents. Where some wives are gregarious and ambitious, others may be shy and retiring. Moreover, each woman has her own limit. For Queen Vashti, arranging a soirée for the women in the town was not too much to ask. But to be requested to parade herself before her husband's guests was.

And for her refusal, Vashti's opportunities seemed to come to a dead end. Like one of her predecessors — another royal woman in the book of Exodus who had gone against the orders of male authority, her father, the Pharaoh of Egypt — Queen Vashti deliberately disobeyed the king's order. For this, she would lose her crown, if not her life.

In the case of the Pharaoh's daughter, the life of Moses was saved and, in turn, a whole nation was saved (Exodus 1:22-2:10). However, in the case of Vashti, a younger, more attractive woman was chosen for the king; a woman who was, the king and his wise men presumed, more obedient. The second queen's name was Esther.

Esther, too, saved the life of her nation.

It is not insignificant that it is through Queen Esther's memoirs that we even hear of the courageous queen by the name of Vashti. If Queen Esther had chosen to ignore the memory of the woman who preceded her on the throne, Queen Vashti might have been lost to history. (It was certainly unlikely that King Ahasuerus would have mentioned his first wife and her disgraceful behavior in *his* memoirs!)

But the king's second wife, Esther, had much for which to thank Vashti. King Ahasuerus might not have been so predisposed to forgive Queen Esther her brazen disobedience had not his first wife taught him that, like it or not, some women will make their own decisions. At least with Esther, the king was willing to hear her out.

By including Queen Vashti's story in her memoirs, Queen Esther set a precedent that we, like she, have a responsibility to our fallen leadership.

We have a responsibility to remember, celebrate, and come to the aid of those women who once gave of themselves on our behalf, but who, for whatever reason — be it divorce, death of husband, or political defeat — now no longer occupy positions of leadership.

We cannot afford to forget or trample on our feminine leaders of the past.

As sisters, it is our responsibility to remember the women, both single and married, who have worked to clear and pave the way for us, at the risk of health, sanity, comfort, reputation, family, and marriage.

If the truth be told, we today are who we are — if we are anybody — because some woman, somewhere, stooped down long enough that we might climb on her back and ride piggyback into the future.

Ask Queen Esther.

Questions for Thought

1. Was there a "better way" for Queen Vashti to have responded to her husband, a way less uncompromising and defiant, that might have saved her her crown?

2. Do men who have been married more than once make better husbands? If so, in what ways?

3. How do you feel when women who are married to men of importance are accorded certain privileges (special leadership posts, priority seating, and the like) simply on the basis of their marriage? For example, pastors' wives?

4. Evaluate the pros and cons of using terms such as "First Lady" and "Queen of the Church" as titles for wives of pastors and other women of renown in the church.

5. Is there opportunity in your church to honor those women and men who have made important contributions to the life and ministry of the church?

6. Strangely enough, widows of famous men rarely remarry. How do you think their lives fulfill them so that remarriage is less of a necessity? For those widows interested in remarrying, what kinds of society pressures do you think make remarriage difficult?

7. For the wife of a pastor who prefers to live a private life, which means abstaining from any active participation in the church, how can we as women in the church not infringe upon her right to choose to live so?

8. As a divorcée and the ex-wife of a public figure and a woman banished to what was, in all likelihood, a remote part of the kingdom, what kinds of adjustments do you imagine Queen Vashti had to make to her new situation?

9. Is there a ministry to divorcées in your church? What kind of hardships do you suppose that divorced women, particularly those women who find themselves divorced after many years of marriage, experience? How can the church minister to its divorced membership?

UNBEGRUDGED BLESSINGS

Read: Luke 1:5-56

Even before he was born, Jesus was changing the lives of women.

While he was on earth, Jesus' ministry profoundly challenged society's restrictions upon women's roles in the religious sphere. But even the preparation for his birth brought about a change in the way women looked at themselves.

To begin with, two women — Jesus' mother, Mary, and her kinswoman Elizabeth — specifically learned what it meant to be blessed women, women chosen by God to be instruments through whom perfect redemption would come into the world.

To be chosen by God is a humbling experience. To be used by God is an awesome experience. To be blessed by God is a joyous experience. . . most of the time.

To prepare for their blessings, Mary and Elizabeth first had to come to grips with the irony of blessedness: namely, that behind every blessing there is burden. Their blessings changed the course of each of their lives forever. Their blessings altered each woman's perception of herself. And, more importantly, being singled out by God as mothers of redemption made them need one another all the more.

Each blessing brought its own lesson.

The first lesson to be learned was how to receive a blessing no longer expected.

In walks Elizabeth.

She had grown accustomed to barrenness. Menstrual cycles she could depend on and uninterrupted sleep through the night had always been a part of her life. Now that she was an old woman,* past the age of having to worry about stained garments and strange female odors, Elizabeth had long given up believing in the miracle of children for her.

"Some blessings we outgrow," she thought. "Others we grow too old to remember."

After all, she had grown accustomed to barrenness.

She had also grown accustomed to what God *had* given her: a devoted husband of many years, Zechariah, whose career as a temple priest brought Elizabeth a reasonable degree of economic comfort and social standing in the community. As the wife of a priest, Elizabeth was a prominent woman. She knew, of course, that behind her back the townswomen ridiculed her, as they did all women without children. But, fortunately, Elizabeth was old enough and wealthy enough to be left alone.

"Besides," she mused, "some disappointments you eventually learn to live with."

Still, Elizabeth was thankful for the one blessing in her life: old age. It was a blessing not many women in her day lived to experience. Few women lived beyond their thirties,

---

*While the text speaks of Elizabeth as being an old woman, she may have been only between her thirties and forties. We know that she was unable to conceive and presumably had passed the age when women typically bore children. How long women menstruated back then, we do not know; but we do know that having started their families typically when they were still young adolescent women, as many women in Eastern cultures still do, many often did not live into their forties.

dying from the complications of (too many) childbirths, or from the sheer exhaustion that came from the unrelieved toil of caring for a household. The lack of proper medical care only exacerbated the problem. The female body remained such a complex, frightening, and mysterious mechanism that men knew only one way to protect themselves against it, and that was to create laws regarding when it was to be touched and when it was to be avoided.*

So Elizabeth had grown accustomed to barrenness.

She had even grown accustomed to the vacant cavity at the base of her uterus. She had grown accustomed to the aching of her uterus whenever she overheard women at the well or in the market place chattering about toddlers' first steps, toothless smiles, and the cost of weddings these days.

But Elizabeth no longer confused the vacant space with barrenness. To her, the vacant space within her was simply another one of the tormenting reminders that she was an old woman.

"Besides, how do you miss something you never had?" she wondered.

Oh, Elizabeth had once prayed for a family, a son, a child. How she had prayed! Like barren women before her, Elizabeth had petitioned God, indeed bargained with God. Like Hannah before her (I Samuel 1:28), Elizabeth had promised to give the child back to God for service in the temple, like his father, Zechariah. If only God would grant her a child.

And she had pleaded: If it was because of an unknown sin in her life that God withheld fruit from her womb, then surely for the sake of her husband, a faithful servant in the temple, God would have mercy. Elizabeth fasted, tithed, kept the Sabbath, observed the Passover, and tried to live a righteous life.

---

*See, for example, the purity laws in Leviticus 12:1-8, 15:19-30; as well as other laws governing men's behavior toward women, such as Leviticus 18:6-23; Deuteronomy 22:13-30, 24:1-4, 25:5-10.

But when her praying yielded nothing, she consulted doctors, quacks, conjure women, charlatans, and soothsayers — anyone who held out promises to wombs closed by God.

What they could not do for her, time did. As far as Elizabeth was concerned, she had learned the most difficult lesson life had to teach: she had learned how to live with unanswered prayers. If she could learn to live with God's silence, she thought, she could live through anything.

But that was before the angel Gabriel brought the news to her husband, Zechariah, that their prayers had been answered.

> "Do not be afraid, Zechariah, for your prayer is heard, and your wife, Elizabeth, will indeed bear you a son, and you will call his name John" (Luke 1:13).

That was before she had to learn how to live with answered prayers and blessings that were long overdue.

Now Elizabeth was with child. But she was more than just pregnant. She was pregnant with a special child, the one who would prepare the hearts of women and men for the Messiah.

> "And you will have joy and gladness,
>   and many will rejoice at his birth;
> because he will be great before the Lord,
>   and he will drink no wine nor strong
>   drink,
> and he will be filled with the Holy Spirit,
>   even from his mother's womb.
> And he will turn many of the children of
>   Israel
>   to the Lord their God...
> to make ready for the Lord a people prepared"
>   (Luke 1:14-17).

Now Elizabeth had to grow accustomed to the blessing growing inside her womb. She had to grow accustomed to fertility in old age. Elizabeth had to learn how to live with unexpected blessings, blessings she had long since stopped looking for, praying for, and desiring.

How do you look forward to something you've never had? How do you live with the blessing of fertility when you have grown accustomed to the curse of barrenness? How do you receive something you've stopped looking for? How do you open a chapter you thought was closed?

For five months Elizabeth hid herself in her house, afraid of and perplexed by the burden of the blessing growing in her womb. Who would understand how she felt? The women around her thought something was wrong with her. Why was she sad and depressed? Had not God blessed her womb — and with a son, no less? Had not God provided an heir for her husband? Had not God granted her someone who would care for her in her older age?

After all, Elizabeth had grown accustomed to barrenness.

Elizabeth was supposed to be happy. "You will have joy and gladness," the angel had said. But all she felt were fear and bewilderment. And there was no one with whom she could talk.

The second lesson to be learned was how to receive a blessing that caused more problems than it solved.

"How can this be?" the words kept going through Mary's head as she sat in her chambers on another side of the country.

Mary was poor and unmarried. And the angel's strange greeting continued to haunt the young woman.

> "Hail, O Favored One! The Lord is with you!
> You are blessed among women!" (Luke 1:28).

"What does it mean to be 'blessed'?" Mary asked in her heart. "How can something be a blessing when it raises more questions than it answers?"

Like her kinswoman Elizabeth in Jerusalem, Mary had to come to grips with the sometimes inconvenience of blessings. She could feel the strange blessing gestating inside. How could this be? How would she explain such a thing? How could she make her fiancé, Joseph, understand that she had not betrayed him, that the child growing inside her was of the Holy Spirit? How *could* this be?

The angel had said to Mary:

> *"Do not be afraid, Mary, for you have found favor with God. And, behold, you will conceive in your womb and bear a son, and you will call his name Jesus"* (Luke 1:30-31).

Mary — a peasant girl, unmarried and untutored — was to be the mother of the Christ.

To be pregnant is one thing.

To be pregnant with the Christ is something altogether different.

How could this *happen?* This was not the way Mary had planned her life.

"How do you defend a blessing you cannot explain?" she asked herself. "How do you live with a blessing that creates more problems than it solves?"

Besides, who would believe her? Joseph? Absolutely not. The townswomen? Hardly. Elizabeth, her relative? Perhaps.

> *"And, behold, your kinswoman Elizabeth in her old age has also conceived a son; and this is the sixth month with her who was called barren"* (Luke 1:36).

At least Elizabeth was married. Still, Mary needed someone to talk with. Someone who knew what it meant to grapple with God's intentions. Someone. A woman, pregnant like herself. Mary's mind kept going back to the old woman Elizabeth. Suppose her kinswoman did not believe her? It was a chance Mary had to take. She needed to talk with another woman.

In pregnancy we are profoundly aware of our womanness. We understand in ways never possible before what it means not to be a man, what it means to be more than a man.

When we are pregnant, we become profoundly sensitive to our bodies. We become conscious of the changes taking place within us: the tingling sensation that eventually turns into human movements; the constant urge to urinate; the bad taste in the mouth in the mornings; the stretchmarks across the belly; the swollen ankles and tender breasts. Let us not forget the fatigue, the overwhelming desire to sleep through it all.

It is a time of contradictory emotions: expectations and apprehension, happiness and depression, confidence and nagging insecurities. The most ambivalent feeling of all is the peculiar craving for contact with other women, especially pregnant women. We are both drawn to pregnant women out of our need to feel normal and repulsed by them because of the seeming abnormality of it all. But the need to feel normal in what is otherwise an awkward, if not ridiculous, posture is the strongest. One word of genuine support from another woman can make an unbearable day livable.

Pregnancy — or whenever our bodies are mysteriously changing — is a time when we search out other women.

* * *

> "In those days Mary rose up and went
> immediately into the hill country, to a city
> of Judah, and entered the house of Zechariah
> and greeted Elizabeth" (Luke 1:39).

There is no way Mary could have anticipated Elizabeth's response. It was one thing to have heard the strange greeting, "You are blessed among women," from an angel: it was haunting. But it was another thing altogether to hear those words from the lips of her older kinswoman: the same greeting made all the difference in Mary's soul. Coming from an older woman of Elizabeth's status — from a woman who had spent much of her life in service to God — the greeting confirmed for Mary the magnitude of the miracle God was performing in her life.

In fact, Elizabeth greeted Mary not only with enthusiasm, but with gratitude:

> "Why is this permitted me, that the mother
> of my Lord visit me?" (Luke 1:43).

Mary was surprised. As the younger of the two, it was she, Mary, who was supposed to show deference to Elizabeth. But the look on Elizabeth's face told Mary that the older woman knew: Elizabeth knew Mary's blessing and she knew Mary's burden.

Filled with humility and gratitude, Mary knelt and embraced her older kinswoman.

If it had not been for the oppressive weight on her feeble legs, Elizabeth probably would have knelt to kiss the younger woman's feet. That she, Elizabeth, should be granted the blessing of meeting the mother of the Christ was more than she could have ever expected.

Even the child in Elizabeth's womb leapt for joy.

Perhaps, on the surface, Elizabeth would have had every reason to envy Mary, the young unmarried woman.

Elizabeth was the elder of the two, the wife of a prominent priest, a God-fearing woman who had prayed all her life for a child. Surely *she* was the better choice to be the mother of the Christ.

Elizabeth's humanity would have told her that she had every right to be jealous. She had the opportunity to quash the young woman's confidence, to invalidate her blessedness. With the younger woman on her knees, distraught and looking up at Elizabeth with pleading eyes, Elizabeth had the opportunity to influence Mary's decision about her pregnancy, the opportunity to influence Mary's image of herself. Yet the older woman did not begrudge her younger unmarried kinswoman the blessing that was Mary's alone.

God's choice was Mary, not Elizabeth.

The young woman kneeling before Elizabeth had been blessed in a most unusual manner. Because of the child growing in her womb, Mary's name would be known throughout history. And Elizabeth knew that her own child would never be as great as the child Mary was carrying. Elizabeth knew, she understood, and she accepted this.

Elizabeth was old enough to know not to contend against the Almighty. So, for the honor of being in Mary's presence, the older woman was grateful. It was an honor Elizabeth could live with.

Seeing the younger woman with the lines of worry etched on her young face, Elizabeth knew that she herself had a lot for which to be thankful. While Mary's blessing may have appeared to exceed Elizabeth's, the older woman had lived long enough to know that "to whom much is given, much is required" (Luke 12:48). The child whom Mary carried would bring Mary much joy, but even more sadness. Mary would be his mother, but he would never be her son . . .completely. So Elizabeth was grateful for what she had.

Elizabeth took Mary's face in her hands and kissed the younger woman's forehead. She knew that both of them had some difficult days ahead of them. And she knew that they would live through them. Somehow, as blessed women, their destinies were bound together.

Heartened by Elizabeth's encouragement, grateful to be with someone who would listen to her story, understand her fears, and celebrate the blessing with her, Mary thanked God for Elizabeth. The young woman threw her head back and sang at the top of her voice:

> "My soul magnifies the Lord, and my spirit rejoices in God, my savior, for God has looked upon the low estate of a hand-maiden...for God who is mighty has done great things for me..." (Luke 1:46,47,48).

Mary's song was not a boast. It was a hymn of praise, sung out of a profound sense of thanksgiving. She sang not just for herself, but for Elizabeth...and for every woman who has ever wondered how to tell God, "Thank you."

To show her gratitude, Mary stayed with Elizabeth until the older woman's ninth month of pregnancy (Luke 1:56).

What the two women talked about, we can only imagine. No doubt they shared stories about the changes their bodies were undergoing. They probably touched one another's protruding bellies and massaged one another's swollen feet. They certainly laughed...and cried...and reminisced...and dreamed. And they most likely imagined the kinds of men their sons would grow up to be.

The two women shared with one another things they could never share with the men in their lives. They held on to one another for dear life. They were women trying to grapple with the hand of God in their lives, sharing with each other the blessedness and the burdensomeness of being blessed.

Elizabeth advised Mary on how to go back and face her confused yet devoted fiancé, how to encourage and love him through the difficult times the two of them faced. Elizabeth shared with the younger woman the secrets of how to live with and through public scorn and whispers, how to hold one's head up with pride in the midst of sorrow.

In turn, Mary gave Elizabeth the strength the older woman needed to carry on during the last months of pregnancy. She helped Elizabeth with the cleaning, cooking, and marketing. Mary's infectious, youthful spirit helped Elizabeth recapture a part of life Elizabeth had long since surrendered to old age and barrenness. Elizabeth remembered what it was to hope, to look forward to something new, to live in expectation.

Finally, what the two women gave to one another was enough to nurture another generation. For what was shared in those three months between them, the two shared also with their sons.

Because his mother was secure about who she was in relationship to Mary and who she was in the sight of God, Elizabeth's son, John the Baptist, was also secure about who he was in relationship to Jesus, Mary's son. Like his mother before him, John accepted the fact that he was not the one chosen by God to be the Light (John 1:1-8).

> "This is the testimony of John, when the Jews sent priests and the Levites from Jerusalem to ask him, 'Who are you?'
> John confessed — he did not deny, but confessed — 'I am not the Christ....'
> 'Then why do you baptize, if you are not the Christ, nor Elijah, nor the prophet?'
> John answered them: 'I baptize you with water; but among you stands one whom you do not know, even he who comes after me,

> *the thong of whose sandal I am not worthy*
> *to untie'* " *(John 1:19-20, 25-27).*

The ministry of Elizabeth's son, John the Baptist, was to confess and bear witness to the Light.

Yet, for the privilege of witnessing and experiencing the presence of God in his lifetime, John, like his mother, was grateful.

Likewise, because of his mother's example, Jesus was touched by the sacrifice and support of his kinsman John the Baptist (Matthew 11:7-15).

> "When Jesus came from Galilee to the Jordan to John to be baptized by him, John wanted to prevent him saying, 'I ought to be baptized by you, and yet you come to me?'
>
> But Jesus answered him, 'Let it be so now; for thus it is expedient for us to fulfill all righteousness.'
>
> And John consented" (Matthew 3:13-15).

Jesus recognized in his kinsman a man unmatched in his commitment.

> "Truly, I say to you, among those born of women there has risen no one greater than John the Baptist" (Matthew 11:11)

To both their mothers' credit, John the Baptist and Jesus grew up respecting one another's ministry. Their mothers' examples also taught them to build on the strengths of one another. And like their mothers, Elizabeth and Mary, before them, in the end both men would learn that there is a price for being blessed.

Questions for Thought

1. We all feel envy at times. How can we keep it under control and prevent it from driving us to destructive behavior?

2. In what ways do parents unknowingly encourage competition and jealousy within and among siblings? Is there anything wrong with competition and ambition? When do they become destructive emotions?

3. How old is a woman when she is "too old to have a child"? Consider this question from both a biological and cultural point of view. What are the emotional and physical problems of having a child when one is significantly older than the norm?

4. Do you know women who have not had children? What are society's attitudes toward these women? How do they feel about themselves? Consider the many ways in which women without children, and women past their childbearing years, may fulfill their desire to nurture children.

5. What are the problems young couples face when they enter into their marriages with a child on the way?

6. One of the women in your church has lost her bid for a position of great responsibility in the church. You have noticed that her attitude has grown bitter and disagreeable since the election. She is particularly bitter toward the woman who was elected, and she goes out of her way to undermine the woman's leadership. If she was your friend,

how would you approach her about her behavior? If, however, you are the woman who was elected, how would you handle this woman's attitude and behavior toward you?

7. In a society like our own which is distinguished by its obsession with competitiveness, in what ways can women prevent competitive behavior from destroying relationships? What is the difference between competing and striving toward excellence?

MY DAUGHTERS, MY SELF

Read: Genesis 19

My Dear Daughters,

Perhaps now I can say to you with my pen what I had for a long time wanted to say with my lips but could not. There was so much silence, so many unresolved issues, so much tension between us when I was alive. Some things not even time can heal. And to lose one's mother to an unknown sorrow is one of them. So, I write you this letter not to explain why I as your mother left you. Some things cannot be explained. Instead, I write to talk to you about why I as a woman had to go somewhere else...

The last time you saw me, I was crumbling before your eyes.

You remember, don't you?

The angels had come to us in the middle of the night, urging us to flee for our lives, warning us against looking back. I remember grabbing both your hands, running for my life, running away from Sodom, praying that I could get the two of you out of there in time, wondering to myself exactly what it was we were running from. No one ever said why we were fleeing. Not your father. Not even the angels. I was just told to flee. And so I fled — with the two of you by my side.

I will never forget that night.

We only had a few minutes left before the city would have been completely consumed with fire. A blazing ball was already lighting the sky from a distance. Your father was yelling threats and curses from outside the window where he was strapping down the mule. The two of you were crying and clinging to one another, pleading with me not to make you leave. I remember looking around and wondering how I could be expected to stuff thirty years of living into one bag. I didn't want the two of you to see me crying. And I knew that you were watching me, studying me through your tears. For once, I wanted you to see me strong. I wanted my daughters to know that their mother didn't always fall apart under pressure.

So I dashed from one side of the room to the other, stuffing everything — anything — I saw into the bag in my arms, all the while singing a ditty I no longer remember. Anything to keep my mind off of what was happening to us. Anything to drown out the sound of your crying and the sound of the ugly screaming voices whispering in my head.

The more I stuffed, the heavier that bag grew, the more my arms ached — until the bag burst and its content spilled about my feet. Without thinking, I found myself stooping to stuff the spilled things back into the torn bag. I remember reprimanding myself — much like your father, or my mother, would have scolded me — for not being more neat. At first I chuckled. Then I began laughing. Soon I could not stop. I could feel your eyes on me. I could sense your horror at what I was doing. But I could not stop myself from laughing, singing, and kneeling there in the middle of the floor. I could almost taste your fear as you watched me, your mother, on my hands and knees singing a strange ditty. . .calmly, methodically, neatly arranging things in a bag that would not comply. . .all the while the world was on fire.

I don't know how long I knelt there, how long you sat there crying and watching me, before the angels came and snatched us away.

In the beginning I didn't know whether to be afraid or to be grateful. I just knew how to be obedient — obedient to your father and obedient to angels in the middle of the night. Believe me: I wanted to ask. I wanted to know what exactly we were running from, where we were going, how long would we have to stay. I wanted to ask, but I couldn't. I could not question your father's judgment. Such things simply were not allowed women in Israel. And so I ran because I was told to run. And though the two of you protested, fought against it, and cried at first, I knew that eventually you, too, would run — because your mother ran.

I've often asked myself why the two of you resisted coming along. Was it because you did not want to leave the friends, lovers, and memories you had collected in Sodom? Or was it because you were ashamed — or afraid — of your mother and did not want to spend the rest of your life with a woman whom you didn't know? Which was it, my daughters?

I know how much I embarrassed you. I know that your friends teased you about your crazy mother. I know what people said about me behind my back.

I know why you both stayed around the house so much: you had agreed that when one of you went on an errand, the other would stay and watch me. You didn't want me to walk the roads alone, talking to myself, laughing to myself, barefoot and going nowhere in particular. You, my daughters, were ashamed of me.

That's also why you never brought your friends home, wasn't it? That's why you learned to lie with a straight face: you didn't want anyone to know that your mother didn't have a mind of her own.

It's hard for me to remember things sometimes. But I

remember how embarrassed the two of you were that day I poured the wine into the well.

It had been an especially hot day and, after much fighting between the two of you, you had decided to bring me along to help with the marketing and carrying water. Your father's uncle Abraham and his family were coming to visit the next day from Hebron, and there was so much to do that one of you couldn't be spared to sit home with me. But if I was to go along, you had decided that noon time was the best time to go. After all, no one shopped or drew water in the middle of the day. It was too hot. There was sure to be no one around to see you, to see the two of you with me.

Surprisingly, that was one of our best afternoons together, you remember, my daughters? It was one of my happy days. Our mule was laden with goat's meat, lentils, and wine from the market. We laughed, sang, and skipped all the way to the well. But when we arrived at the well outside of town, some of your friends were milling about. I knew you were nervous. So I pretended not to notice that your smiles had frozen on your faces. I pretended not to notice that your arms quickly dropped from my waist. One of you mumbled under your breath. The other gasped. I decided to take the pails from your hands and pretend to be occupied with cleaning them with my dress tail. Although everyone's eyes darted over toward me throughout the time, eventually you and your friends started up a conversation that took your attention away from me.

I remember standing there in the sun, admiring my daughters as they stood smiling nervously in a circle with friends, talking quietly but easily. I was always shy around people. I was so proud of the two of you standing there with your friends, I wanted to make you happy and wanted you to be proud of me. So I thought I would draw the water from the well myself and save us some time.

It wasn't until I heard someone scream that I knew something was wrong.

Later that evening I overheard the two of you crying and telling your father how I had opened the six skins of wine and poured the wine into the well.

There was a drought that summer, wasn't there, my daughters?

Mothers know when they embarrass their daughters. We know it, because we were once daughters too. Sometimes we embarrass our daughters deliberately. But most times we can't help it. Sometimes I would look into your eyes and see my own reflection. I would see myself at your age: young, supple, energetic, excited, and full of dreams. Other times I would look into your eyes and see the woman I had become: old, withdrawn, disoriented, unpredictable, and tired — so, so tired.

Oh, I know I'm not the mother you wanted. My mother was not the mother I wanted. But I am the mother you have. And I did the best I knew how. And that's all I could give you, my daughters: the best I knew how.

I gave birth to you the best I knew how. Even though I nearly died on the birthing stool with both of you. I remember that the midwife kept telling me to push. But evidently I was pulling instead of pushing. I guess I didn't want to let go of you; I knew that we'd never be as close again as we'd been those nine months.

I tried to nurse you the best I knew how. Even though my milk never would come and both of you had to nurse on goat's milk.

I tried to care for you the best I knew how. Even though I always forgot your names and cried all day each time one of you was on your menstrual cycle.

I tried even to love you the best I knew how — which was the hardest part of all. I tried, my God, how I tried.

Oh, my daughters, I loved you, to be sure. But I didn't love you the way you wanted, needed to be loved. I loved you the way broken women tend to love — brokenly. And not to be loved the way you want and need to be loved is, I suppose, worse than not being loved at all. So, rather than love you in the broken way I knew how, I kept my love for you to myself. Instead, I complained, lashed out, criticized, withdrew, and stared blankly.

But I didn't mean to hurt you. I just meant to protect you. I suppose I didn't want you to become like I was. I didn't want you to ask too much of life, only to have your spirit wither away when life reneged on your dreams. I didn't want to hurt you — but I would if I had to. Because I knew that if you could live with the hurt a mother inflicts, you would be able to withstand the disappointments that life brings.

So, I guess you could say, I didn't fight to keep my mind. I had no reason to do so.

After all, you girls were always your father's daughters. Because I was sick for months after both of you were born, and because I was frequently ill while you were growing up, the burden of raising you and tending to your needs fell upon your father. Fortunately, your father never really complained. He was proud, smart, dependable, and stubborn about his convictions. Your father was everything your mother was not. And he loved the two of you, in his own way, the way a father loves daughters who he wishes were sons. The three of you were so close that I often felt like an object of humiliation, a distraction — like a disfiguring scar on an otherwise smooth layer of skin. And to pay you back for not talking to me, for not inviting me to share in your secrets and revelry, sometimes I would invite the women in my mind to keep me company.

Your father said I was crazy. He said I was an unfit mother, a poor excuse for a wife. Your father never loved me enough to be ashamed of me; he just contented himself with despising me. At least that is the way he acted. Still, your father never left me. Which for a woman in this society, my daughters, is better than being loved. Your father was good enough not to divorce me (though the voices in my head said he was too cruel to divorce me). Divorce was certainly his prerogative as an Israelite man married to an unstable woman. Nor did he take the two of you away from me — not physically, anyway.

So, even though your father had his bad ways, nevertheless, he was a good man, I suppose. He didn't leave me, nor — despite the advice of his family and friends — did he take you away from me. He kept me and was good enough to remind me of the things I was always forgetting. . .the most important being what a deranged woman I was.

When I wasn't sick, I was a good mother. You remember how I'd sing to you when you were afraid? But when I was sick, I was a living terror. I stayed in bed all day long, refused to comb my hair or wash my body, forgot to cook, rocked myself back and forth, and threw things at the two of you when you talked above a whisper. I can still hear your little feet tip-toeing across the room, your little voices whispering outside my door as you drew lots to see which one of you would be responsible for telling me that it was time for evening prayer.

Sometimes when you were young, I would watch the two of you playing, and before I could heed the tug on my heart at the sight of you playing quietly, contentedly, the voices inside me would start screaming all kinds of ugly things for me to do to you. That's why I would start screaming sometimes without warning: I was trying to drown out those ugly voices, trying to make them shut up. I didn't mean to frighten you, I just wanted the voices to go away.

Both of you think I never noticed your efforts to console me, don't you? You think I was too cussed mean to appreciate the lengths you'd take to preoccupy me, too melancholy to notice your attempts to distract me from my illness. And you're right — in part. You're right that there were many times when I was too absorbed in my own agony to respond to your expressions of concern and affection. You're probably also justified in thinking me cruel when I screamed at you, slapped you without cause, and stared absently at you when you'd plead with me to respond. But what you wanted from me, needed from me, my daughters, was never mine to give. Sometimes a child's needs are so strong, her demands so relentless they choke at you; they threaten to snuff out the little life you try desperately to hold on to. I was having problems enough just trying to be a woman; and you two were pulling on me to be a mother. The two of you wanted me to give you something I'd never had. Which, to me, was cruel of you.

Because I had the problems I had, no one ever took me seriously. Your father certainly never did. The people in the town ignored me. You all thought I didn't know. But I knew.

The part that hurts the most, however, is that even in death, I am ignored. No one even bothered to record my name on my obituary. It reads like a postscript, a parenthetical aside:

> "By the way, his wife looked behind her, and
> she became a pillar of salt" (Genesis 19:26).

Just because a woman is sick doesn't mean she doesn't want to live.

Although there are many things that remain elusive to me, one thing is imprinted in my memory: As we were fleeing Sodom, I remember the looks on both of your faces when you saw me collapse before your eyes — your expressions of horror, bewilderment, contempt.

The two of you are mad because I looked back, aren't you? After all, the angels commanded us not to look back. And you think I deliberately looked back just to be ornery, just to be hateful, don't you? You think I intentionally took my life to make you all feel guilty for the rest of your lives, don't you?

I didn't.

My looking back had nothing to do with you, my daughters.

As we were running out of Sodom, I got to thinking. I started seeing my whole life. The smell of death will make you do that, you know. I saw my life as a nervous child, my years as a neurotic woman, my marriage as an obedient wife, my parenting as a forlorn mother. I thought about the things which had happened to me in my life, the things which I'd let happen to me. For some reason, I especially remembered my mother punishing me by sealing me in a cave all day while she went about her errands. I remembered my father slapping me unconscious one day when I sneaked in to touch one of the holy scrolls. (I later discovered that, while I was still unconscious, he beat me because he found out I had touched the scrolls while I was on my menstrual cycle.)

As we were running, I remember thinking about the fact that I didn't even know why I was running. Oh, Lot had said something about Sodom being destroyed. But I didn't quite know why. Why must a whole city be destroyed for the sins of few? More importantly, why were *we* being saved? Why *this* family? Where were we going? How did we know we could survive in the lonely hills? How did we know we could love one another in a deserted place? What would it take to start over?

Must the voices in my head go where I go? Who would keep me company should the voices depart? Why did I have to give up everything to be saved? Without a mind to call my own, what was I being saved for?

The more we ran, the more questions I asked.

How far must I run before I know I am safe? Would safety give me back my mind? Was my problem spiritual or was my problem geographical?

At least the three of you would have memories of Sodom. Something to get you through the loneliness of what lay ahead. I never had more than the present moment. At any time, I could forget all the things I'd finally learned to ask.

I thought if I could just get a glance at what I was leaving, a portrait to tuck away in my mind amidst the other clutter and images strewn there, perhaps when the time came to start over, I would have something in my mind to let go of. I thought that if I was to be healed, I needed to be sure I knew what had made me ill. I just wanted to see exactly how far I had come.

So, no matter what they may say about your mother, my daughters, remember: I didn't look back, I just looked around.

Questions for Thought

1. Reflect on the feelings you had as you read this story. What emotions were most strongly evoked?

2. Reflect on your relationship with your own mother. With what parts of this mother's story can you identify in your relationship with your mother? Which parts are most unlike your relationship? What is your most fond memory of your time with your mother? What is your most unpleasant memory of your time with one another? Have the two of you ever discussed these incidents? If not, what keeps (or kept) you from sharing your memories?

3. Reflect on your relationship with your own daughter(s). With what parts of this mother's story can you identify in your relationship with your daughter(s)? Which parts are most unlike your relationship? What is your greatest wish for your daughter(s)? What is your greatest fear for your daughter(s)? In what ways are you and your daughter(s) alike and unlike?

4. If you had to do it over again, what as a mother would you do differently in rearing your daughter(s)?

5. If you had a choice in the matter, would you choose your mother to be your mother? If not, whom have you met who epitomizes the kind of woman you would choose to be your mother?

6. In what ways, if any, do relationships between daughters and mothers differ from those between daughters and fathers?

7. Do you know anyone — whether due to illness or any other reason — who is unable to show love? What is the nature of your relationship with that person? What are some of the ways in which we can communicate love and caring to someone absorbed in his/her own pain?

8. More times than we care to admit, we observe members of our churches, communities, and circle of friends gradually unravel emotionally before our eyes. How can we support them and their families through such crises? What are the institutional resources that are available within your church or community?

9. What is mental illness? How does mental illness differ from emotional illness? Why do you think women constitute a greater proportion of those diagnosed as mentally and/or emotionally ill?

10. Do you know anyone with a mental illness? What is your relationship with that person? What is your greatest frustration in that relationship? What are the positive things to be gained in such a relationship? What kind of fears does this society manifest regarding mental illness?

BIBLIOGRAPHY

Andolsen, Barbara. *Daughters of Jefferson, Daughters of Bootblacks: Racism and American Feminism*. Macon, GA: Mercer University Press, 1986.

Andrews, William L. *Sisters of the Spirit: Three Black Women's Autobiographies of the Nineteenth Century*. Bloomington, IN: Indiana University Press, 1986.

Atwood, Margaret. *The Handmaid's Tale*. Boston: Houghton Mifflin Co., 1986 / New York: Ballantine Books, 1987.

Davis, Angela Y. *Violence Against Women and the Ongoing Challenge to Racism* (Freedom Organizing Series #5). Latham, NY: Kitchen Table Press, 1985.

Fiorenza, Elisabeth Schuessler. *In Memory of Her: A Feminist Theological Reconstruction of Christian Origins*. New York: Crossroads Press, 1984.

Giddings, Paula. *When and Where I Enter: The Impact of Black Women on Race and Sex in America*. New York: William Morrow & Co., 1984.

Klatch, Rebecca E. *Women of the New Right*. Philadelphia: Temple University Press, 1986.

Lorde, Audre. *The Cancer Journals*. New York: Spinster, Inc., 1980.

———.*Sister Outsider*. Trumansburg, NY: Crossings Press, 1984.

Lowenberg, Bert, and Ruth Bogin. *Black Women in Nineteenth-Century American Life*. University Park, PA: Penn State University, 1976.

Mandela, Winnie. *Part of My Soul Went With Him*. New York: W. W. Norton & Company, Inc., 1985.

McNamara, JoAnn. *A New Song: Celibate Women in the First Three Christian Centuries*. New York: Harrington Park Press, 1985.

Miller, Jean Baker. *Toward a New Psychology of Women*. New York: Beacon Press, 1977.

Mitchell, Ella P. *Those Preachin' Women*. Valley Forge, PA: Judson Press, 1985.

———. *Those Preaching Women, Vol. 2*. Valley Forge, PA: Judson Press, 1988.

Mollenkott, Virginia. *Godding: Human Responsibility and the Bible*. New York: Crossroads Press, 1987.

Moltmann-Wendel, Elisabeth. *The Women Around Jesus*. Translated by John Bowden. New York: Crossroads Press, 1980.

Moltmann-Wendel, Elisabeth, and Jurgen Moltmann. *Humanity in God*. New York: The Pilgrim Press, 1983.

Mudflower Collective. *God's Fierce Whimsy*. New York: The Pilgrim Press, 1985.

Pobee, John S., and Barbel von Wartenberg-Potter, eds. *New Eyes for Reading: Biblical and Theological Reflections by Women from the Third World*. Geneva: World Council of Churches, 1986.

Rich, Adrienne. *Blood, Bread and Poetry: Selected Prose 1979-1985*. New York: W. W. Norton and Company, Inc., 1986.

Rollins, Judith. *Between Women: Domestics and their Employers*. Philadelphia: Temple University, 1985.

Scanzoni, Letha, and Nancy A. Hardesty. *All We're Meant to Be: Biblical Feminism for Today*. (rev. ed.). Nashville: Abingdon Press, 1986.

Sterling, Dorothy, ed. *We Are Your Sisters: Black Women in the Nineteenth Century*. New York: W. W. Norton and Company, Inc., 1984.

Stokes Brown, Cynthia, ed. *Read From Within: Septima Clark and the Civil Rights Movement.* Navarro, CA: Wildtrees Press, 1986.

Toor, Djohariah. *The Road by the River: A Healing Journey for Women.* San Francisco: Harper & Row, Publishers, Inc., 1987.

Walker, Alice. *In Search of Our Mothers' Gardens.* New York: Harcourt Brace Jovanovich, Publishers, 1983.

———. *Revolutionary Petunias and Other Poems.* New York: Harcourt Brace Jovanovich, Publishers, 1973.

Walker, Margaret. *Jubilee.* Boston: Houghton Mifflin Co., 1966.

Williams, Delores S. "Womanist Theology: Black Women's Voices." *Christianity and Crisis,* Vol. 27, No. 3 (March 3, 1987) 66-70.

Women Under Apartheid. London: International Defence and Aid Fund for Southern Africa, in co-operation with the United Nations Centre Against Apartheid, 1981.

Nashormeh Wilkie, illustrator

Nashormeh Wilkie is a visual artist and Coordinator of Community Services for the Baltimore Museum of Art, Education Department. Her involvement in art has led her to teach art in the Philadelphia public schools, to work as an archivist, to specialize in arts and crafts in community centers and museum centers, and to paint public murals — in such diverse places as Philadelphia, Camden, and Jamaica. Currently, Ms. Wilkie lectures in African American art history at the Community College of Baltimore and in city public schools.

Renita J. Weems, author

Renita J. Weems is an Assistant Professor in Old Testament Studies at Vanderbilt Divinity School in Nashville, Tennessee, and an ordained elder in the African Methodist Episcopal Church. A former economist, public accountant, and stockbroker, she is also a free-lance writer, with numerous articles published in *Essence*, *MS*, and *SAGE*. She is currently a Contributing Writer for *Essence Magazine*. Her nationwide ministry includes teaching, writing, speaking, preaching, and leading seminars.